WHAT MAKES A GREAT PRESIDENT?

STEPHEN TRYON

WHAT MAKES A GREAT PRESIDENT?

Names: Tryon, Stephen, author.
Title: What makes a great president? / Stephen Tryon.
Description: [Milwaukee, Wisconsin] : Accountability Citizenship, [2024] | Includes bibliographical references
Identifiers: ISBN: 979-8-9898145-1-0 (print) | 979-8-9898145-2-7 (ebook) | LCCN: 2024917093
Subjects: LCSH: Presidents--United States--History. | Political parties--United States--History. | Presidential candidates--United States. | BISAC: POLITICAL SCIENCE / Political Process / Political Advocacy. | POLITICAL SCIENCE / Political Process / General.
Classification: LCC: E176.1 .T79 2024 | DDC: 352.230973--dc23

Copyright © 2024 by Stephen Tryon

ISBN 979-8-9898145-1-0
Library of Congress Control Number: 2024917093

All rights reserved. No part of this book may be reproduced in any manner whatsoever without written permission except in the case of brief quotations embodied in critical articles and reviews.

First Printing, 2024

CONTENTS

Preface vi
Dedication xii

1 Introduction 1
2 Experience Factor Analysis 5
3 Why The Best Are The Best 13
4 Why The Worst Are The Worst 39
5 Five Legacy Addresses 61
6 Welcome to the Seventh Party System 87
7 Conclusions and Observations 99

Works Cited 113

Preface

The President of the United States is our country's Chief Executive, and the head of one of the three co-equal branches of our government. Under the Articles of Confederation, the first government of the United States did not have a Chief Executive. Whether to have a Chief Executive, and how much power to entrust to the office, were hotly debated during the 1787 convention that produced the United States Constitution. The delegates to that convention had different views on many issues, from slavery to how to raise and spend federal currency to the relative power of the states versus the federal government. They were united, however, in their respect and trust for George Washington, the man they elected as the president of the constitutional convention. The respect and trust for Washington, and the expectation that he would be first President of the United States, were certainly major factors in the establishment of the executive branch as it is defined in Article II of the Constitution. There is a word for the constellation of attributes that can inspire that type of respect and trust: that word is character. In writing a book with the title *What Makes a Great President?*, the easy answer is that great presidents have the right character. The purpose of this book is to explore what the right character is and is not, precisely, as it has been manifest in the behaviors of the best and worst presidents of the past two-hundred and thirty-four years.

The Honorable Max Cleland (Aug 24, 1942- Nov 9, 2021) was a Soldier and a distinguished public servant. On April 8, 1968, while participating in combat operations during the Battle of Khe Sanh, Captain Cleland was grievously wounded in a tragic grenade explosion. He lost both legs above the knee and his right arm. After a lengthy recovery period at Walter Reed Army Medical Center, Max returned home to Georgia. From that point, his career as a public servant included time as a Georgia State Senator, the head of the United States Veterans Administration under President Carter, Georgia's Secretary of State, United

States Senator, and Secretary of the American Battle Monuments Commission.

I had the privilege of serving as a Fellow in Senator Cleland's office in 2001. During that year, and for the last twenty years of his life, he taught me a lot about American government and the character of public service. Some of the teaching came from books he would give me, some came through the opportunity to work with him on various projects, but most came from watching him serve while bearing the relentless burden of his wounds with grace and dignity. His service improved the lives of veterans, of anyone in need who crossed his path, and of those of us who worked with him.

September 11th, 2001, started like many other days during my tenure in Senator Cleland's office. A 6AM train ride from Virginia into Washington, D.C., a cup of coffee, and a review of the news stories from the "Early Bird"—a daily compendium of stories from major news sources around the world that would be of interest to United States' defense and government leaders. The main event on my schedule for the day was also the first event on Senator Cleland's calendar: I was "staffing" his meeting with incoming Chairman of the Joint Chiefs of Staff, General Richard B. Myers, USAF.

General Myers was meeting with all members of the Senate Armed Services Committee in preparation for his confirmation hearing. The Chairman of the Joint Chiefs is the principal military advisor to the President. The traditional round of meetings with key legislators allowed for identification and resolution of any issues that might stand in the way of a speedy confirmation.

I had prepared a memorandum for Senator Cleland a few days prior, outlining General Myers' distinguished career and summarizing the key defense interests directly affecting the people of Georgia. Georgia is an important state for our nation's military, with significant elements of the Army, Navy and Air Force residing within the state's borders. These interests were second nature to Senator Cleland, and the summary served more to remind him of any recent activity affecting the state due to ongoing base realignment, procurement and budgeting, or organizational initiatives.

The meeting was scheduled to start at 9:00 AM, so at about 8:45 I walked to the elevator where I expected Senator Cleland would arrive. General Myers, his aide, and a legislative liaison officer from the joint staff arrived first, around 8:50 AM. We exchanged introductions, and they asked if I had heard about the plane hitting the building in New York. They had just received initial reports about an aircraft hitting one of the towers of the World Trade Center a few minutes earlier. I had not heard this report, as I had been away from my desk getting ready for the meeting. General Myers was concerned, and we discussed how, from the first reports he had, this seemed to be a different order of magnitude from the small private plane that had hit a building in Florida several months earlier. Senator Cleland arrived, and we moved quickly into his office and started the meeting a little early.

Senator Cleland proceeded quickly and told General Myers he had read his bio, and that he considered Myers a brother because they had both served in Vietnam. Then he said something I will never forget. It only took him a minute or two, and I think it is the most perfect statement I have ever heard of what we should expect from our elected government officials in terms of taking care of the people they serve. To the best of my recollection, it went something like this: "Now general, when you come over here and ask to send American troops into harm's way, I am going to ask you hard questions. I want you to know why. I have read [former Secretary of Defense] McNamara's book *In Retrospect*, and in that book I read where he had concluded the war was unwinnable by 1967. Now I was a young tiger in 1967, and I had heard President Kennedy say years before 'Ask not what your country can do for you but what you can do for your country.' I volunteered to go to Vietnam. So I had to ask myself, if McNamara knew the war was unwinnable, why the heck did he sign my orders and send me over there? Because frankly, general, the war didn't turn out so good for me. So when anyone asks to send American troops in harm's way, I will ask hard questions because it's my job to make sure we don't send any of our young tigers into a war we don't think we can win or a war we don't have to fight. I take that responsibility very personally."

General Myers acknowledged that he, too, took his responsibility for the lives entrusted to his care very seriously. I just had time to think, "Wow, this is exactly the kind of conversation Senators should have with the incoming Chairman. It was so much more important than the summary of state defense issues I included in my memo." Then cell phones and beepers started to go off, and the aide came in and told us the news: a second plane had hit the World Trade Center. The United States was under attack. General Myers left immediately, and within a short while we were instructed to evacuate our offices.

As I worked on this book, contrasting good presidents with those who performed poorly, Max' comments to General Myers frequently came to mind. There is something essential in that exchange between two Americans sworn to support and defend the Constitution. The Constitution is the social contract between the American people and its government, designed to fulfill the promise of the Declaration of Independence: that proper governments are instituted to protect the rights of the people they serve, including the rights to life, liberty and the pursuit of happiness. Our government must act for the good of all of us, including defending all of us from very real threats, but we expect it to do so in a way that is respectful of the rights of each of us. That is hard stuff; it is natural that we should have differences of opinion on what must be done and on how to go about doing it.

It is natural that we should have differences of opinion on what must be done and on how to go about doing it. The Constitution gives us peaceful, legitimate processes to resolve those differences of opinion. Our system includes checks and balances, and we have peaceful, legitimate processes for modifying existing laws. Our Chief Executive, the President of the United States, must have the character both to maintain the legitimate processes that are the foundation of our government and to maintain the trust of the people in those processes. More than any other single individual, the President balances what must be done for all of us with the price that is paid by each of us, ensuring that the government's actions for the collective good are sufficiently respectful of the rights of individuals.

Max loved history, and often had historical anecdotes to inject into a conversation. So, for instance, when I read about the difference between Hoover's handling of the veterans' "Bonus Army" protests in Washington, D.C. in 1932 and FDR's handling of the same protests the following year, I thought of Max. The Hoover administration provided no support to the veterans and eventually sent in troops to clear out their encampment, killing two veterans and a child (Brands 258-59). FDR had a camp built for the veterans, complete with mess halls and latrines with showers. He sent Eleanor Roosevelt and his special assistant Louis Howe to meet with the veterans. Eleanor related how she had visited the trenches in France during the war, and how she respected what the veterans had done there. She and Howe joined the veterans for a meal, and later led them in singing songs from the war years (Brands 330-31). In neither case did the veterans get the early payment of the bonus they wanted, but the way they were treated by their government was the difference between a violent confrontation and a peaceful end to the protest.

Max was the "FDR type" public servant. His wounds were a powerful reminder of the price of our freedom. He had the ability to unify people across the political spectrum, in part because he reminded them that, even when we are doing what we must for the benefit of all of us, we have a duty to ensure government is properly respectful of the rights of each of us. On multiple occasions, I witnessed the Republican Chairman of the Armed Services Committee call on Senator Cleland, a Democrat, to comment on some issue in order to remind all present of the higher purpose both parties were seeking: balancing the good of all with the good of each within the constraints of our peaceful, legitimate processes of government.

Like all our greatest elected leaders, Max strove to make everyday Americans feel their government worked for them. This election, in 2024, will be my first presidential election in some time without Max' counsel. For the past five presidential elections, I have had the benefit of his observations on the issues and the character of the candidates. As I finished this book, therefore, it seemed appropriate to dedicate it to Max. Without his influence and example, I probably would not have written it.

For Max Cleland
A mentor and friend who exemplified the best character of public service.

The author with Secretary Cleland.

CHAPTER 1

Introduction

This book presents four sets of facts that will help you make a wise choice when voting for President of the United States. While not specific to any particular presidential election, the facts presented here should be helpful not only in reaching your decision this year, but also in articulating intelligent reasons for your vote. The four sets of facts are (1) an experience factor analysis to identify job experiences (or the lack thereof) that correlate with presidential greatness and presidential weakness, (2) an analysis of our four greatest presidents to identify what made them great, (3) an analysis of our four worst presidents to identify what made them poor presidents, and (4) five famous speeches made by our greatest presidents. Chapter Six, "Welcome to the Seventh Party System" provides a summary of the evolution of our party system over time before defending the proposition that we entered a Seventh Party System in the 1990s. At the end of the book, the conclusion section of Chapter Seven summarizes the lessons from the first six chapters and distills what we have learned about our best and worst presidents into a generic scorecard suitable for any presidential election. In the observations section of Chapter Seven, I offer my view of how the scorecard should be filled in for the 2024 election.

The reader can extract benefit from each of the four sets of facts presented here without necessarily reading the entire book, or even entire chapters. Chapter Two contains graphical depictions of the main points of the experience factor analysis. Chapters Three and Four contain illustrations that summarize the takeaways from each of our four greatest and four worst presidents. Each of the presidential addresses in Chapter Five are of great value as stand-alone pillars of our American Republic: they are rich in inspiration and perspective.

Chapter Six is one of two places in the book where, in addition to the factual description of the evolution of the first six party systems, I defend an opinion: the proposition that we have been living in a new, Seventh Party System shaped by the internet and deregulation of radio and television. The main characteristic of this Seventh Party System is an electorate that is overloaded with information and misinformation, and that, to a large degree, lacks the tools to process information effectively at the scale required for effective citizenship. Many people fall back on outdated and dogmatic paradigms to simplify decisions like how to vote. For many, one of these paradigms is a party identity that may be more of a family legacy than the product of active, constructive reasoning. The significance of Chapter Six to the overall purpose of the book is simply to highlight the importance of using the facts presented in chapters two through five when deciding how to vote, rather than relying on a party identity that may be out of date.

The main emphasis of this book is, as described above, four sets of facts. The selection of any set of facts is, of course, somewhat subjective. The facts as presented here represent a reasonable assessment of past presidents and a sound rubric for choosing among a field of candidates.

That said, it is incumbent on me to offer my opinion on how this rubric should apply to the candidates for president in the 2024 general election. The "Observations" section of Chapter Seven contains that assessment, which, of course, is the other place in the book where I defend an opinion. I encourage readers to read the factual portions of the book and to make your own assessment on this year's election before reading the "Observations" section of Chapter Seven.

So, at last, what makes a great president? The analysis in Chapter Two shows that the experience factors that correlate most strongly with presidential greatness are experience as a vice president in a previous administration and experience as the governor of a state or territory. Conversely, lack of prior experience in an elected public office is the factor that correlates most strongly with bottom-tier performance as president. Chapter Three tells us that our greatest presidents unified the Americans of their day, led our country's successful response to the greatest challenges of their time, and left a powerfully positive legacy for future generations. Chapter Four illuminates the characteristics and traits associated with our worst presidents: they engage in rhetoric and support policies that encourage division and violence, they fail to meet the major challenge of their term in office, and, in many cases, they participate in or tolerate corruption, bribery and theft in government. Finally, the words of our greatest presidents in Chapter Five inspire Americans of all times to dedicate themselves to "the great task remaining before us... that, government of the people, by the people, for the people, shall not perish from the earth" (Lincoln, "The Gettysburg Address").

CHAPTER 2

Experience Factor Analysis

Major businesses don't choose their senior leaders randomly. Neither does the American military. In both cases, successful organizations develop senior leaders by assigning them to preparatory jobs in which they develop key skills while performing essential tasks. As we prepare to choose a new Chief Executive of the United States, we should all understand what history teaches us about the resume most likely to make a great president. Here is the bottom line: experience as a vice president in a prior administration or as a governor of a state or territory are more likely to make a great president than any other type of experience, while presidents with no prior experience in elected office are more likely to rank in the bottom tier of all presidents.

This chapter compares experience factors--jobs held before becoming President of the United States--with four different publicized rankings of the forty-two people[1] who served as president through George W. Bush. The goal is to provide a simple guide to the specific job experiences that correlate with better or worse performance as president.

Most credible sources agree on the general ranking of our presidents. In other words, even though scholars may disagree on the exact rank of individuals within the list of all presidents, there is significant consensus on who is in the top and bottom third of American Presidents. Using four different rankings from distinct organizations over the past twenty years provides some mitigation for the inevitable difference between specific rankings and for changing perceptions over time. The rankings used here are from CSPAN (2021), the American Political Science Association (APSA, 2015), the Sienna College Research Institute (SCRI, 2010), and the Federalist Society / Wall Street Journal (Federalist Society, 2005). Full citations appear at the end of this book to allow readers to examine these sources directly.

This chapter excludes our three most recent presidents from the data set because, frankly, there is simply too much controversy about these current figures to include them without undermining the credibility of the overall analysis. People are deeply invested in their personal beliefs about these men, and it is likely that their terms in office are still too recent to avoid significant bias. It is reasonable to think our view of any public figure becomes clearer and more accurate when we have the ability to consider the value of their service over time. Leaving out the last *three* presidents also allows us to consider a pool that breaks down into three equal tiers of fourteen former chief executives. This simplifies our job-factor analysis and minimizes controversy without materially affecting results.

If you doubt the reasoning behind excluding the most recent three presidents, then consider this fact. The 2005 survey conducted for the Federalist Society and Wall Street Journal ranks George W. Bush (Bush 43), the president at the time of the survey, at number nineteen--slightly above the middle. According to some participants, conservative respondents ranked Bush 43 among the very best presidents while liberal respondents ranked him among the very worst, and this extreme difference of opinion resulted in his average ranking. With more hindsight however, both liberals and conservatives become much more consistent in the general rankings of presidents. Bush 43 is in the bottom half of all presidents in the 2010, 2015, and 2021 rankings in our data set.

Of the forty-two men who have held the office of President of the United States through President George W. Bush, thirty have been college graduates. Twenty-eight have been veterans of military service. Twenty-three served in one or both houses of Congress before becoming president. Twenty-two have studied or practiced law. Eighteen served as governors of states or territories. Fourteen held cabinet posts, twelve were general officers, nine were Vice Presidents in prior administrations *before being elected on their own*, and eight were ambassadors. Four had no prior elected-office experience. We might expect these factors, or, in some cases, combinations of factors, to have affected the quality of job performance as president. For purposes of simplicity, the analysis in this chapter focuses on two job factors that unambiguously correlate with better performance as president: experience as a vice president in a prior administration and experience as a governor. There is also one job factor that clearly correlates with bottom-tier performance as president: the lack of any prior experience in elected office.

The first step to determine if there is a correlation between any given job factor and performance is to calculate the percentage of presidents that shares a particular factor. For instance, as stated above, thirty of the presidents in our data set have been college graduates, and thirty is seventy-one percent of the forty-two presidents in that set. If graduating from college has no correlation to performance, we would expect college graduates to be evenly distributed across the top, middle and bottom tiers of presidents. In other words, we would expect seventy-one percent of the top, middle, and bottom tiers of the population of presidents to be college graduates. Specifically, seventy-one percent of the fourteen presidents in each tier is just a fraction less than ten presidents. Since it makes no sense to speak of a fraction of a president, we round to the closest whole number to get, in this case, an expected value of ten college graduates in each tier. A positive correlation to any tier means a higher-than-expected number of presidents in that tier were college graduates. A negative correlation means a lower-than-expected number of presidents in that tier were college graduates.

Correlation is not causation. To say a positive correlation exists between a factor and a ranking does not mean the factor causes the ranking. A positive correlation means that the presence of a particular factor makes the correlated ranking more likely. A negative correlation means that the presence of a particular factor makes the correlated ranking less likely.

At this point, the analysis is simply a factual discussion of correlations between experience factors and performance rankings within the group of past presidents through our forty-third president. The claim that these historical correlations are likely to hold in the future is an example of inductive reasoning. Inductive reasoning can only establish that an outcome is more or less likely. It does not imply that any future outcome is certain. We use this type of reasoning all the time, however, to make decisions about what we will do in the future. In the financial sector, for example, the standard disclaimer that "past performance is not a guarantee of future results" does not keep us from using past performance as one of our decision factors for how to invest. In a similar fashion, the correlations discussed here should be considered but one factor in a comprehensive evaluation of candidates.

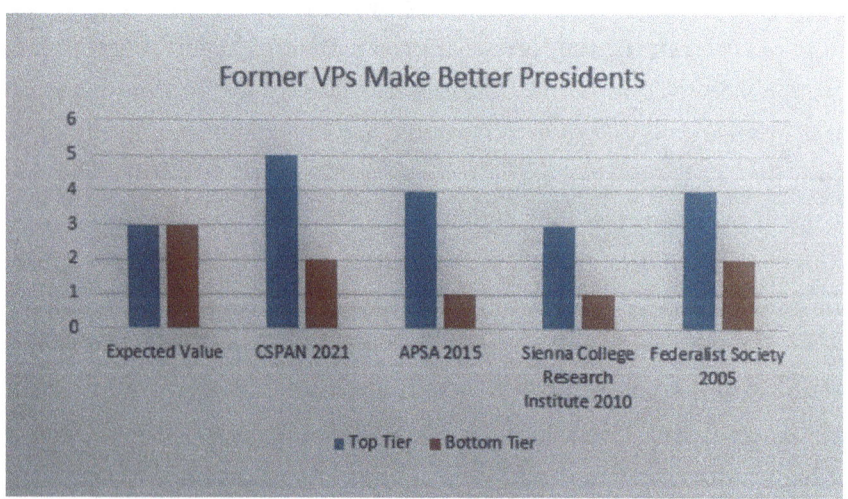

Historically, one of the two experience factors most likely to result in a top-tier president (among presidents elected in their own right) is serving as the vice president in a prior administration. In the set of presidents through George W. Bush, there have been nine individuals who served as vice president in a prior administration before winning their own elections to become president. Nine is twenty-one percent of the forty-two presidents in our data set. If prior experience as vice president was neutral with respect to performance as president, we would expect an even distribution of these people across the top, middle and bottom tiers of presidents. Since we are only considering presidents through George W. Bush, each tier consists of fourteen presidents. Therefore, if experience as vice president has no effect on performance as president, we should see twenty-one percent of fourteen, or three presidents from our subset of former vice presidents elected in their own right, to appear in the top and bottom tiers. However, in three of the four surveys, four or five of the nine presidents in this subset ranked in the top tier of all presidents. The fourth survey had the expected number of three in the top tier. In all four of the surveys, only one or two of the presidents from the former-vice-president subset appeared in the bottom tier. So their is both a positive correlation for top-tier performance and a negative correlation for bottom-tier performance in this subset. Former vice presidents later elected as president are more likely to be top-tier presidents and less likely to be bottom-tier presidents than we would expect if vice-presidential experience was performance-neutral.

The other experience factor that unambiguously correlates to top-tier performance as president is prior experience as governor of a state or territory. The pool of presidents in our data set includes 18 former governors--that is forty-two percent of the forty-two men who served as our country's chief executive through Bush 43. If serving as a governor before becoming president did not affect performance as commander-in-chief, we would expect to find six prior governors in both top and bottom tiers. Six is forty-two percent of the fourteen presidents in each tier. However, two of the rankings--CSPAN and the Sienna College Research Institute (SCRI)--had seven former governors in the top tier, and the Federalist Society ranking had eight. Only the APSA ranking had the expected value of six former governors in the top tier. The data shows a positive correlation for top-tier performance among former governors serving as president.

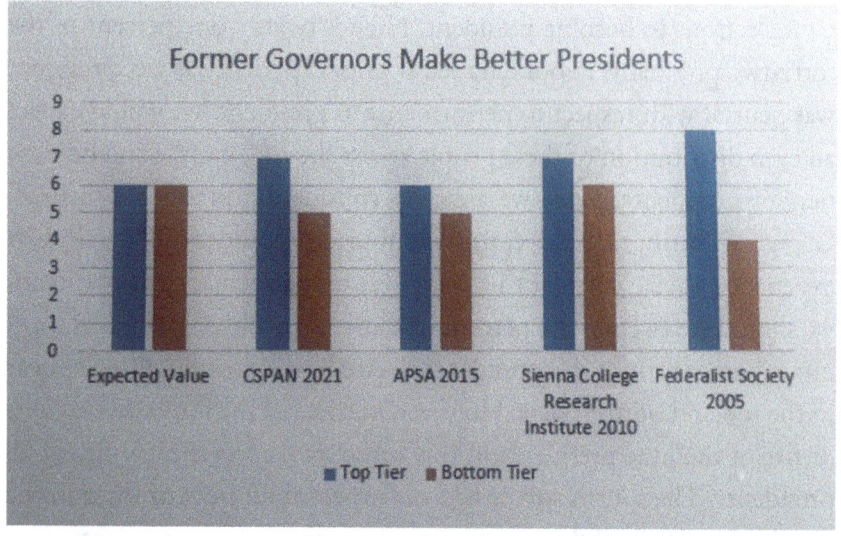

Not only did prior experience as a governor make it more likely for past presidents to be top-tier, but three of four surveys also showed that presidents with prior experience as governors were less likely to be ranked in the bottom tier of all presidents than we would expect if governorship was a performance-neutral factor. Two surveys (APSA and CSPAN) had five former governors in the bottom tier of presidents. The Federalist Society survey had only four. The SCRI survey alone had the expected number of six former governors in the bottom tier. We can infer from this historical data that candidates with experience as governors are more likely to perform better than average while in office.

As we might expect, candidates who lack prior experience in an elected office are more likely to be bottom-tier performers as president. The number of presidents in our data set who have entered office with no prior elected-office experience is just above nine percent. That translates to an expected value of one in both top and bottom tiers. Three of the rankings used in our analysis have two of these presidents in the bottom tier while the fourth ranking has three. This indicates a definite correlation to bottom-tier performance among presidents with no prior elected-office experience. The only president without elected-office experience who ranked in the top tier (in all four rankings) was President

Eisenhower, who of course had significant experience as a senior military officer leading an international coalition of forces in World War II.

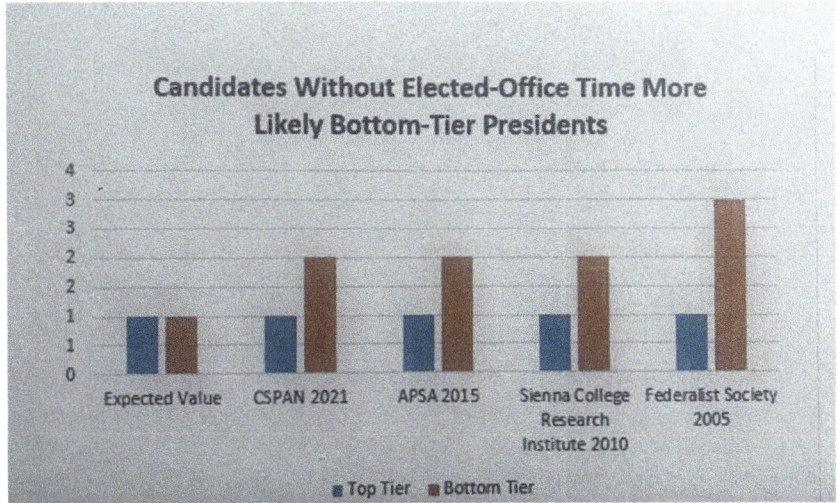

History tells us that candidates with a certain type of experience--experience as a vice president in a prior administration and experience as a governor of a state or territory--perform better as president of the United States. Likewise, we can see from the performance of past presidents that those without experience in elected office are more likely to be bottom-tier performers when thrust into our country's top elected office. In a time when there is so much misinformation in the characterizations of current events, this experience-factor analysis is a helpful aid to making the best choice. In the next chapter, we look at the specific histories of our greatest presidents in order to find other signs of presidential greatness.

---

[1]President George W. Bush was the 43d President of the United States, but because President Cleveland served as both the 22d and 24th President, "Bush 43" was the 42d person to hold the office.

CHAPTER 3

Why The Best Are The Best

All four rankings used for this book list Abraham Lincoln, George Washington, and Franklin Delano Roosevelt (FDR) among the top four American presidents. Three of the four rankings list Teddy Roosevelt (TR) among the top four. The Federalist Society 2005 ranking places TR as the fifth greatest president, and is the only survey in our data set to put Thomas Jefferson in the top four. In the order in which they served as president, this chapter examines the historical context, presidential achievements, and legacy of the four people most consistently ranked as the four greatest American presidents: Washington, Lincoln, TR and FDR. These presidents rank so highly because they united the Americans of their day, they led our country's successful response to the greatest challenges our nation has faced, and they left a powerfully positive legacy for future generations.

George Washington: The First President (1789-1797)

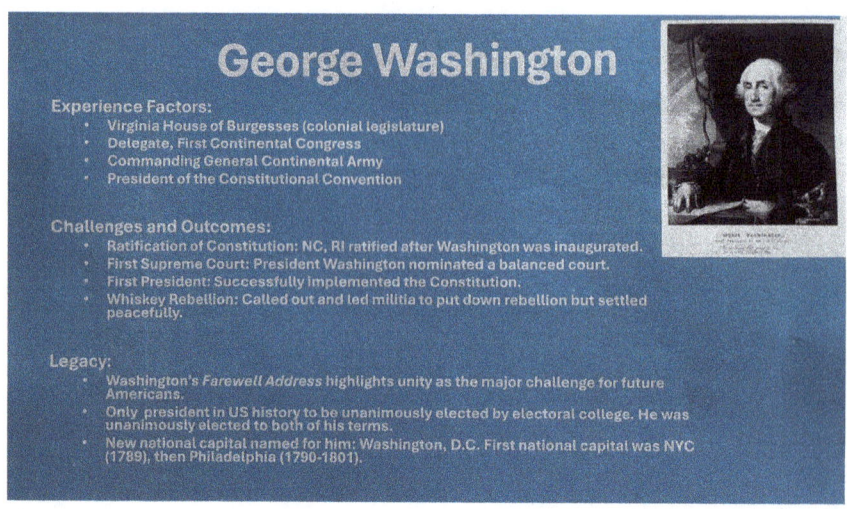

Historical Context: 1781-1789

It is difficult to separate George Washington's contributions in the years leading up to his election as our first President from his contributions in that role. Indeed, the United States might not have survived its first government, under the Articles of Confederation, without Washington's influence and example. During this period, Washington defused a potential mutiny by the Continental Army, surrendered his commission as Commanding General of the most powerful military force in the United States, hosted the Mount Vernon Conference, and served as President of the Constitutional Convention.

In 1783, the weak central government under the Articles of Confederation could not pay the Continental Army for several months. The Army was quartered in Newburgh, New York, awaiting the signing of the Treaty of Paris that would formally end the American Revolution. A group of politicians and officers conspired to have the Army present an ultimatum to Congress threatening a coup. Washington intervened, unexpectedly showing up at the meeting where the matter was to be discussed. He asked to address the gathering. His personal address to his officers requesting their continued loyalty to Congress defused the potential mutiny and reinforced the principle of military subordination to civilian authority in the United States.

Later that year, the Treaty of Paris formally ended the American Revolution. Washington requested of Congress the details of how he should resign his commission. Congress formed a committee to establish those details, which were designed to emphasize the power of Congress over the military. Washington remained as Commanding General of the Army until the last British troops left New York in November, and tendered his resignation to the Congress of the United States at the Maryland State House in December. When King George III was told that Washington was going to voluntarily give up his command, he remarked that, if he did this, "he would be the greatest man in the world."

Almost immediately after the end of the American Revolution, the weaknesses in the Articles of Confederation--the framework of the first central government of the United States of America from 1781 to 1789--led to serious problems with the regulation of commerce between states. One area of concern directly affected George Washington, who owned land on the border of Virginia and Maryland, as well as further west. Washington hosted a conference with delegates from the two states at Mount Vernon. This conference recommended similar meetings for states to resolve issues of commerce between the states. This process eventually led to Congress authorizing the Philadelphia Convention that produced the United States Constitution.

Washington was part of the Virginia delegation in Philadelphia, and was unanimously elected as President of the Constitutional Convention. A legendary warrior, landholder and frontiersman, Washington was likely the only person known and trusted enough to oversee the process of forging a new framework for the national government. At the outset, the divisions among the delegates seemed insurmountable. Federalists versus anti-federalists, slaveholders versus abolitionists, big states versus small states, and rich versus poor: each fault line created challenges that had to be reconciled in a structure that could balance competing interests, protect individual liberty, govern effectively, and win sufficient popular support to be ratified by the states. Through it all, Washington's steady hand assured that the delegates' efforts would yield a draft constitution that could be put before the people with a reasonable chance of successful ratification.

The Presidency of George Washington

Once the Constitution was ratified, the election of Washington as our first president was a foregone conclusion. The greatest challenge facing the new American government was the challenge of unity. The same divisions that threatened the success of the Constitutional Convention persisted and threatened the survival of the country. Certainly, Washington's ability to serve as a point of unity among conflicting factions is one reason he is considered a great president.

The fact that Washington was unanimously elected for both his first and second terms confirms that, for his contemporaries on all sides of the many contentious issues of the day, his presence was essential to preserve the unity of the young republic. Ten states participated in the 1789 election and there were sixty-nine electors representing these states. New York state did not have electors in place for the election. North Carolina and Rhode Island had not yet ratified the Constitution. Washington received sixty-nine electoral votes. Four years later, with one-hundred-thirty-two electors representing fifteen states, Washington was re-elected with 132 electoral votes. He is the only president to ever be elected unanimously by the electoral college. Certainly, the broad trust in Washington across the entire spectrum of conflicting political factions is the reason he was able to unify different elements.

Washington correctly focused on the long-term unity of the republic as he managed philosophical differences within his cabinet, addressed foreign policy concerns, and created the institutions that had been sketched out in the Constitution. His appointed all six justices that comprised the first Supreme Court, and his appointments included three people from northern states (John Jay of New York, James Wilson of Pennsylvania, William Cushing of Massachusetts) and three from southern states (John Blair, Jr. from Virginia, John Rutledge of South Carolina, and Robert Harrison of Maryland). When Harrison declined his appointment for health reasons, Washington nominated John Iredell of North Carolina to take his place. Washington's cabinet appointments reflected a similar concern for creating a sense of connection to the central government for citizens of different regions. During his two terms as President, Washington's court and cabinet appointments included sixteen people from eight states. History shows that Washington's focus on unity was a correct assessment of the greatest threat of his time, and his efforts in shaping the institutions of the federal government helped give our young republic an essential period of unity that lasted more than sixty years.

The most direct challenge to the unity of the United States during Washington's tenure as president was the Whiskey Rebellion, a revolt by farmers in western Pennsylvania against taxes on distilled spirits. Farmers distilled excess crops into whiskey and rum because it did not spoil, it was easier to transport, and it served as a medium of exchange. Congress passed a tax on distilled spirits to help pay down debt from the Revolutionary War. Some farmers rebelled and many simply did not pay the tax. In response to an attack on a tax collector, President Washington called on governors to provide militia to suppress the rebellion. Washington himself rode with a militia force of about 13,000, but also sent mediators to negotiate a peaceful settlement with about 600 farmers who had taken up arms. Some were arrested and later pardoned. President Washington's handling of the rebellion is generally considered to have strengthened the unity of our country by demonstrating its ability to respond to internal violence while also avoiding unnecessary bloodshed.

Perhaps the most explicit statement of the priority Washington placed on national unity and one of his most enduring contributions to our country is the message of his Farewell Address.

> In contemplating the causes which may disturb our Union, it occurs as matter of serious concern that any ground should have been furnished for characterizing parties by geographical discriminations... whence designing men may endeavor to excite a belief that there is a real difference of local interests and views. One of the expedients of party to acquire influence within particular districts is to misrepresent the opinions and aims of other districts. You cannot shield yourself too much against the jealousies and heartburnings which spring from these misrepresentations (Washington).

We can see the wisdom of Washington's warning in American politics today. The degree of misrepresentation has risen to the level where even the most obvious lies about the 2020 election and about supposed differences between rural and urban Americans are accepted as truth by millions. Washington, therefore, ranks as one of our greatest presidents because of his ability to inspire trust across the political spectrum, for successfully addressing the greatest challenge facing America in his time, and for leaving future generations an accurate guide to the challenges that would persist long after his death.

Abraham Lincoln: The Sixteenth President (1861-1865)

> **Abraham Lincoln**
>
> **Experience Factors:**
> - Illinois Militia / Blackhawk Wars
> - Lawyer
> - Illinois State Legislator
> - Member, House of Representatives (U.S. Congress)
>
> **Challenges and Outcomes:**
> - Civil War: Union victory preserves United States of America
> - End of Slavery: Thirteenth Amendment ends slavery, but domestic terror groups like the Ku Klux Klan effectively deny African Americans the rights of citizenship in America for the next 100 years.
>
> **Legacy:** First Inaugural Address, Gettysburg Address, Emancipation Proclamation, Second Inaugural Address

Historical Context: 1787-1861

When the founders of our country signed the Constitution in September of 1787, nearly 700,000 slaves made up about eighteen percent of the population of the United States. There was widespread recognition that the institution of slavery was inconsistent with the principles of the Constitution, even among some of the people who owned slaves. The ordinance that established the Northwest Territory (present day Ohio, Indiana, Illinois, Michigan, and Wisconsin) in July of 1787 made slavery illegal there. Rhode Island, Delaware, and South Carolina passed laws making the slave trade illegal that same year, but slavery itself remained legal in most states until the Thirteenth Amendment was ratified in 1865.

Historians estimate seventeen to twenty-five of the fifty-five delegates to the Constitutional Convention owned slaves, including George Washington. Some of the other delegates were abolitionists, including Benjamin Franklin. The document the delegates sent to the states was a compromise that protected slavery: the delegates thought that compromise necessary to produce a document that enough states would ratify. Specifically, southern states were given more representation in Congress by allowing them to increase their population by three-fifths for each slave, even though slaves were not given any of the rights and privileges the Constitution bestowed on white men. In addition, the document prohibited the federal government from passing any legislation that restricted the slave trade until 1808.

As the country expanded, Congress continued to struggle with the conflict between pro-slavery and anti-slavery forces. Every new territorial acquisition represented the potential for new states that could alter the balance of power in Congress. The Missouri Compromise (1820), for example, added Missouri as a slave state and Maine as a free state at the same time, while prohibiting slavery north of a specific latitude (36° 30') in the remainder of the Louisiana Territory. The Compromise of 1850 was a package of several laws that allowed California to become a free state, organized the territories of Utah and New Mexico with provisions to allow the population to vote on whether any states formed from these territories would be slave or free, and created a requirement for escaped slaves captured in free states to be sent back into slavery.

The process of using legislative compromises to forestall conflict over slavery broke down when the Kansas-Nebraska Act became law in 1854. This law repealed the Missouri Compromise by replacing the restriction on slavery in the Louisiana Territory with a provision for popular sovereignty while creating the two new territories of Kansas and Nebraska. Pro-slavery and anti-slavery forces rushed into the Kansas Territory to sway the vote, and violent conflict broke out.

The physical battles in Kansas mirrored an intensified social conflict over the issue of slavery across American society. Pro-slavery Representative Preston Brooks used a cane to beat abolitionist Senator Charles Sumner in the Senate chamber of Congress in May of 1856. Sumner almost died. Earlier that same year, a lawsuit by a slave named Dred Scott had worked its way to the Supreme Court. In March of 1857, the Court's ruling denied citizenship to anyone of African descent and ruled that Congress could not pass laws to prevent the spread of slavery (*Dred Scott v. Sandford*). Abolitionist John Brown, hoping to arm slaves and start an insurrection, led a raid on the federal arsenal at Harpers Ferry, Maryland in October of 1859. Brown was captured and executed.

The Presidency of Abraham Lincoln

When the strategy of compromising with slavery fell apart in the spring of 1861, Abraham Lincoln was there to meet the challenge. Lincoln is widely considered our greatest president. He ranks number one in two of the four surveys used for the statistical analysis contained in this book, and he is number two or three in the other surveys. Lincoln ranks among our very best presidents in all the surveys for good reasons: he did everything possible to avoid civil war after his inauguration, he served as Commander in Chief and led the Union to the total victory necessary for preserving the United States, and he left a rich legacy of wisdom to guide the process of national healing that continues, imperfectly, to this day.

In his First Inaugural Address, Lincoln expressly stated that he would not take steps to end slavery in the states where it existed, that he would do what was necessary to ensure the laws of the Union were followed in all the states, and that he would not use force unless it was forced upon him to do so. By the time he was inaugurated (March 4, 1861), however, seven states had already seceded from the Union (South Carolina, Mississippi, Florida, Alabama, Georgia, Louisiana and Texas). Lincoln continued to work for a peaceful solution to the secession crisis for over a month after his inauguration. He did not commit to restoring the Union by force of arms until after the Confederate States began the war by attacking Fort Sumter on April 12. After the war began, four more states joined the Confederacy (Virginia, Arkansas, North Carolina and Tennessee).

Before the attack on Fort Sumter, in an attempt to restore the Union and avoid war, Lincoln offered a constitutional amendment that would have protected slavery in the states where it existed. Though any compromise with slavery seems wrong today, Lincoln was simply offering to codify what had been the policy of the federal government from the Constitutional Convention forward. Washington and other presidents allowed slavery through a series of constitutional and legislative compromises because they believed these compromises were necessary to establish and preserve the United States, and many believed states would eventually abolish slavery on their own.

After the Confederate States attacked Fort Sumter, Lincoln vigorously executed his duty as Commander in Chief. At the beginning of the war, the Union Army had only about 26,000 soldiers and few generals. By May of 1865, it had over a million soldiers. Lincoln taught himself military strategy and was better at it than many of his generals early in the war. Perhaps because a lot of fighting took place relatively close to Washington, but also because he was dissatisfied with the actions of his early commanding generals, he was heavily involved with the planning and execution of the Union military strategy. Lincoln's willingness to study military strategy and tactics, his direct involvement in the military strategy of the north, and his insistence on replacing generals who did not give him victories were essential in defeating the Confederacy and preserving the United States.

The Union Army's most experienced general, Winfield Scott, proved too old and resigned after the first battle in 1861. His replacement, George McClellan, proved too cautious and Lincoln replaced him after the bloody and inconclusive Battle of Antietam in 1862. Lincoln fired a number of other generals for battlefield failures as well: Pope, Buell, Burnside, Hooker, and Rosecrans. Finally, with Ulysses Grant, he found the aggressive fighter who would win the total victory necessary to restore federal control over the states that had seceded. Lincoln's active involvement as Commander in Chief was essential to the Union military victory in the Civil War.

Finally, in addition to his efforts to avoid the war and his essential leadership as Commander in Chief, Lincoln delivered political and motivational messages that gave all Americans a powerful vision of the positive potential of the post-war United States. Besides the immediate importance of these messages, Lincoln's words have provided an enduring source of encouragement and wisdom as our nation continues its process of healing from its bloodiest war and its legacy of racial injustice. From the First Inaugural Address to the Gettysburg Address to the Emancipation Proclamation to the Second Inaugural Address, it is impossible to read or listen to Lincoln's words without being inspired by the potential of a free people governing themselves within the framework of the Constitution of the United States.

> I am loathe to close. We are not enemies, but friends. We must not be enemies. Though passion may have strained it must not break our bonds of affection. The mystic chords of memory, stretching from every battlefield and every patriot grave to every living heart and hearthstone all over this broad land, will yet swell the chorus of the Union, when again touched, as surely they will be, by the better angels of our nature (Lincoln, "First...").

Here, at the end of Lincoln's First Inaugural Address, is the magic not only of Lincoln but of all our greatest presidents. In the darkest of times, our greatest leaders remind us that we have "better angels" and that we will again find better days, if we remain united, if we face our challenges together, and if we use and adapt the brilliant framework we have been given to meet whatever challenges confront us.

Theodore Roosevelt: Twenty-sixth President (1901-1909)

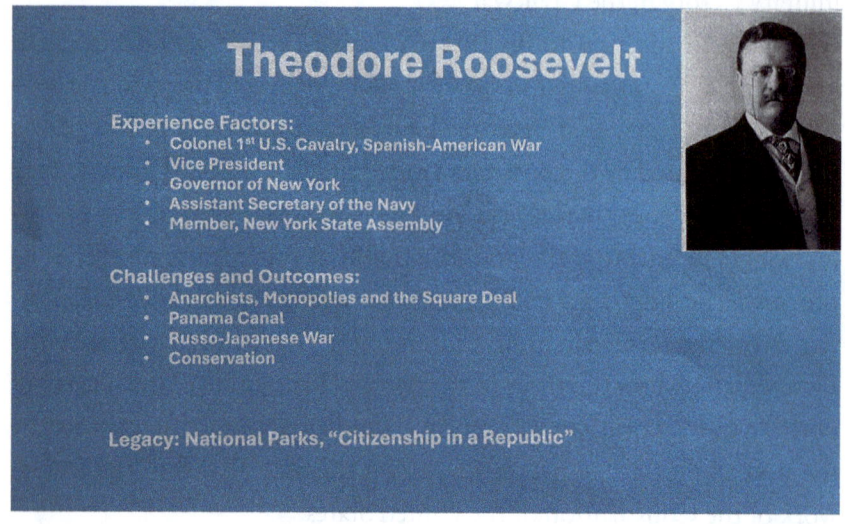

Historical Context: 1840-1901

It is easy to overlook the domestic and international turbulence that characterized the end of the nineteenth century and the beginning of the twentieth. In her classic history of this period, Barbara Tuchman notes that all change prior to the nineteenth century had been evolutionary, but at the end of the nineteenth, revolutionary changes in industry and science had multiplied human capacities "a thousandfold:"

> **Industrial society gave man new powers and new scope while at the same time building up new pressures in prosperity and poverty, in growth of population and crowding in cities, in antagonisms of classes and groups, in separation from nature and from satisfaction in individual work (Tuchman, xv).**

The new pressures Tuchman described were like the shifting of tectonic plates on which the entire world order rested. The shifts caused urgent crises in domestic politics and foreign policy around the globe. These crises created opportunities and challenges for emerging powers like the United States. Theodore Roosevelt ranks among our greatest presidents because of the way in which he united the American people in meeting the challenges and seizing the opportunities that confronted the United States during his time in office.

By the end of the nineteenth century, capitalism and the industrial revolution had created great concentrations of wealth, often by exploiting workers who had been displaced as economies transitioned from mostly agrarian to an industrial base. Telegraphs and newspapers made people more aware of disparities in wealth and poor working conditions. Governments were more responsive to wealthy business owners and often took their side in conflicts with workers. Workers' awareness of these conditions fueled anti-government worker movements like the anarchists and Marxists. Tuchman notes that in the period between 1894 and 1901, five heads of state in five different countries were assassinated: President Carnot of France in 1894, Premier Carnovas of Spain in 1897, Empress Elizabeth of Austria in 1898, King Humbert of Italy in 1900, and President McKinley of the United States in 1901. The anarchist assassins believed governments were perpetuating unfairness and inequality, and apparently thought they were striking a blow for fairness by murdering heads of state.

The Presidency of Theodore Roosevelt

Theodore Roosevelt (TR) became the twenty-sixth President of the United States after the assassination of President William McKinley in 1901. TR's family was prominent and wealthy, descended from a Dutch farmer who arrived in New Amsterdam around 1650 and owned a farm in what is now the middle of Manhattan. His father and grandfather were successful in banking and business. TR was elected governor of New York in 1898. Uncomfortable with the reforms TR was pursuing as governor, powerful New York politicians influenced the Republican convention to nominate him to be William McKinley's vice president in the 1900 presidential election. After serving three and a half years as McKinley's successor, TR was elected on his own ticket in the next election (1904) and served until 1909.

Theodore Roosevelt took positive steps as president—dramatically different from those of his predecessors—to reach across the gulf created by power and privilege in order to unify Americans and avoid social strife. He advocated his "Square Deal" domestic policies to encourage fairness for all citizens, quality standards for food and drugs, and checks on the power of railroads and monopolies over workers. When unionization caused a coal strike in 1902, Roosevelt hosted a meeting between management and labor and acted as a neutral party to encourage a settlement. Previous presidents had generally sided with management to break strikes; Roosevelt's actions thus set a new precedent that could be seen as an effort to address the perception that governments perpetuated unfairness. Theodore Roosevelt also aggressively used the Sherman Antitrust Act to break up large monopolies, like Standard Oil and some railroad conglomerates. He helped make the American economy fairer for working people (Roosevelt, Theodore).

Roosevelt's actions in foreign affairs did more to propel the United States to a position of world leadership than any of his predecessors. He started construction of the Panama Canal, increased the size of the United States Navy, and sent the Great White Fleet to visit ports around the world as a demonstration of American power. Roosevelt brokered the Treaty of Portsmouth to end the Russo-Japanese War in September of 1905, for which he later received the Nobel Peace Prize. He was the first American to win a Nobel Prize. In the international arena, Theodore Roosevelt acted vigorously to protect the interests of the United States and to assert U.S. leadership in solving international problems.

Roosevelt also made dramatic, positive contributions to important, long-term challenges like civil rights and conservation. In the area of race relations, he invited Booker T. Washington to dine with him at the White House shortly after he became President. This dinner provided an example of a leader who understood that the promise of the Constitution applied to all Americans. Roosevelt also demonstrated great foresight when he made conservation a priority. By establishing many national parks, forests and monuments, he reinforced the government's role as a guardian of natural resources for future generations. The problems of civil rights and conservation were certainly too big for Theodore Roosevelt to "solve" in the first decade of the twentieth century. But he leveraged the federal government to make America radically more fair for the working class and led all Americans with a unifying vision of the potential of our Constitution and our vast country.

Franklin Roosevelt: Thirty-Second President (1933-1945)

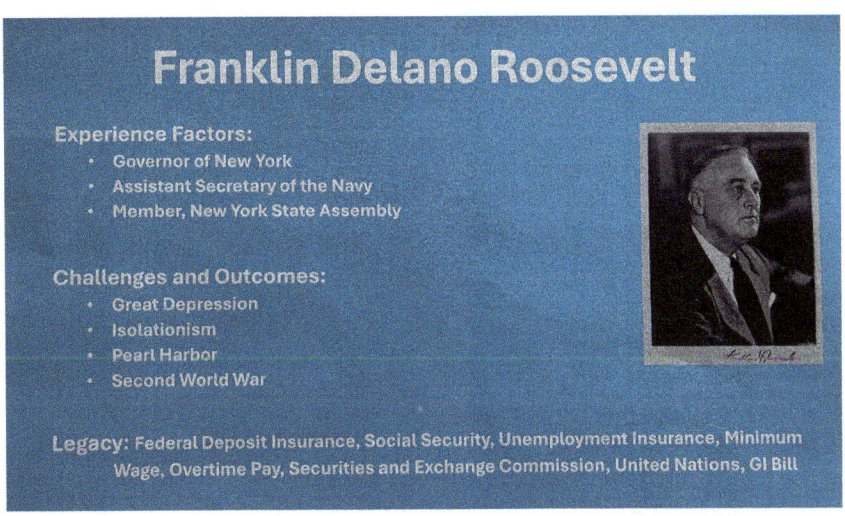

Historical Context 1918-1933

The general election in 1918 was a mid-term election: there was no presidential election until 1920. Election Day was on November 5, just six days before the Armistice ended the First World War. The Republicans took control of the Senate and maintained control of the House of Representatives, giving them the ability to block President Wilson's efforts to build a post-war international community based on free trade and self-determination. Wilson suffered an incapacitating stroke in the fall of 1919. Republican Warren Harding won the 1920 presidential election, giving Republicans complete control of the federal government.

During the twelve years they held complete control of the federal government, Republican policies in both foreign and domestic affairs unwittingly set the conditions for the Depression and the Second World War. In foreign affairs, Republicans favored an isolationist policy. The Republican-controlled Senate rejected the Treaty of Versailles, keeping the United States out of the League of Nations. As the world's strongest economic power, American isolationism doomed the League. European economies struggled with inflation, unemployment and debt. Competition for resources and markets powered an increasingly industrial global economy and encouraged aggression.

At home, the American economy boomed, except for the farm sector. Republicans favored little regulation of an economy that had evolved from almost entirely agrarian to a complex mix of industry, agriculture and finance. Herbert Hoover, the Republican president when the stock market crashed in 1929, had been the Secretary of Commerce since 1921. The lack of economic regulation enabled excessive speculation, unreasonable valuations in the American stock market, and increasing disparity between rich and poor.

In 1928, FDR introduced New York Governor Al Smith to the Democratic National Convention. Roosevelt's speech was broadcast across the country on radio, a relatively new technology that was rapidly gaining in popularity. In a year when it seemed everything was going in favor of the Republicans, Smith became the Democratic candidate. Roosevelt grew his political stature and support because of his convention activities. Smith convinced FDR to run to replace him as Governor of New York. While Smith lost the general election to Herbert Hoover in a landslide, FDR won a hard-fought election in New York state.

When it came, the Great Depression was a nearly complete failure of the largely unregulated capitalist economic system that had sprouted with the industrial revolution. Between September of 1929 and the end of 1932, the Dow Jones Industrial Average (DJIA) lost 89 percent of its value and unemployment in the United States rose to an all-time high of 25 percent. The United States had none of the systems in place that could help absorb these tremendous economic shocks: there was no insurance on bank deposits, no unemployment insurance and no social security system for those too old or disabled to work. Without these systems, many people tried to withdraw what savings they had to meet their needs, creating enormous pressure on banks across the country (Brands 286-87).

Like most businesses at this time, banks were largely unregulated. They sought to earn a profit by investing a portion of the money customers deposited into their accounts. Many banks did not keep adequate reserves, and the stock market crash caused bank investments to lose value along with the market in general. As unemployed people sought to withdraw their savings, thousands of banks did not have enough reserves to meet the demand for cash. Because there was no deposit insurance, when these banks failed, customers who still had money deposited simply lost their money. The fear of losing money on deposit made the problem worse as people rushed to withdraw their money. The combination of unemployment and lost savings led to foreclosures, putting more pressure on banks and making many people homeless.

During the period between the stock market crash and the 1932 presidential election, President Herbert Hoover's administration did not effectively respond to the hunger and homelessness millions of American citizens were experiencing. By relying too much on the private sector and state governments to provide relief, the administration's efforts failed to meet the needs of the people. When the president signed a tariff to shore up prices for agricultural goods, other countries enacted tariffs of their own, causing a collapse in global trade. As the time came for the election of 1932, the vast majority of Americans were looking for a change of direction.

By 1932, Hoover was unpopular and violence was becoming more commonplace. A confrontation between police and unemployed Ford workers led to four deaths and scores of injuries. Organized protests by some farmers became violent as well. When thousands of war veterans, some with their families, assembled in Washington DC to demand early payment of a bonus they had been promised, Hoover opposed the bill to meet their demands. Most of the veterans left at this point. Hoover used the army to clear out the encampment of those who would not leave. Two veterans and a baby were killed in that encounter.

Meanwhile, Roosevelt easily won reelection to the governorship in 1930. As governor of what was then the largest state (by population) in the country, FDR implemented policies that helped millions of New York residents suffering from the effects of the economic collapse. At a special session of the state legislature in 1931, Roosevelt called for the creation of a Temporary Emergency Relief Administration (TERA) to provide material relief to the unemployed. Over the next year, TERA deployed $50 million--some appropriated by the legislature and some raised through a bond approved in a state-wide referendum--to create jobs and provide food, clothing, fuel and housing. By early 1932, with the Hoover administration doubling down on ineffective trickle-down solutions to the crisis, FDR announced that he was running for president.

Roosevelt campaigned on the idea of a "new deal" for the American worker. Like his Republican cousin Theodore Roosevelt, FDR was a progressive. His new deal aimed to use government to regulate America's economy so that it provided better security and quality of life for working people, the elderly and the disabled. FDR won the 1932 election in a landslide, returning Democrats to the White House for the first time in twelve years.

The Presidency of Franklin Delano Roosevelt

Franklin Delano Roosevelt (FDR) served as the 32d president of the United States from the depths of the Great Depression in 1933 until his death in the final months of World War II. He was elected to the presidency four times and is the only president to have served more than two terms. FDR ranks as one of the top three presidents in all four surveys used for this analysis. He successfully united Americans across the economic spectrum to meet the challenge of the Great Depression, and then united Americans with a diverse coalition of nations to defeat European fascism and Japanese aggression in the Second World War.

By the time FDR was inaugurated on March 4, 1933, the economic situation was urgent. In his inaugural address, he acknowledged the seriousness of the problems facing the country, identified the highest priority task as putting people to work, and pledged to treat this task "as we would treat the emergency of a war." He also indicated the need for "a strict supervision of all banking and credits and investments." He expressed confidence that the people of America would come together and overcome the economic challenges facing the country. He called for a special session of Congress to address his specific proposals, and said that he would take whatever steps were necessary to meet the current challenges (Roosevelt, Franklin Delano).

Within days, FDR began to deliver on his promises. He declared a four-day national bank holiday on March 6th. He signed the Emergency Banking Relief Act on March 9th. On March 12, the day before the banks were to reopen, FDR went on the radio and explained to the American people the changes the new law would make to the banking system. Within a week, Americans had returned one billion dollars to their bank accounts. On March 15, the first day of stock trading since the holiday, the Dow Jones Industrial Average recorded its largest percentage gain in history, jumping over fifteen percent. While it would be nearly a decade before the economy was fully recovered, and there were setbacks along the way, FDR's bold action restored the confidence of millions of Americans and put the country on the road to recovery immediately.

Over the remainder of his time as president, FDR's "New Deal" transformed the relationship between the United States government, the business community, and the people in ways that provided a more equitable distribution of the benefits of American society. While not everything he tried was successful or well-received, he worked tirelessly to shape and enact many successful innovations that provided remedies for both the symptoms and causes of the Great Depression. New banking laws provided the first insurance on bank deposits while establishing standards for reserves and other banking activities. The creation of the Social Security Administration in 1935 created a government-backed mechanism, in partnership with business and workers, to fund unemployment insurance as well as pensions for the elderly and disabled. The Civilian Conservation Corps put young unemployed men to work developing and protecting America's natural resources through programs that created hundreds of state and national parks, planted billions of trees, developed America's first ski slopes, and provided both infrastructure and people to fight forest fires and aid in soil conservation. The Tennessee Valley Authority Act created an administrative agency to provide flood control, power generation, environmental stewardship and economic development. The Fair Labor Standards Act of 1938 provided the first federal minimum wage and established standards for overtime pay. Later, after millions of Americans had been drafted to fight World War II, FDR proposed and enacted the first GI Bill, providing WWII veterans funds for college education, unemployment insurance, and housing. No other president's programs have had such a positive and sustained impact on American prosperity as those of FDR's New Deal.

Addressing the effects of the Great Depression here in the United States made domestic policy of paramount importance at the time of FDR's first inauguration, but the global effects of the depression had already pushed much of the rest of the world into an abyss of totalitarianism and aggression that would lead to the Second World War. In the final months of 1931, Japan occupied the Chinese province of Manchuria and installed a puppet government there. When the League of Nations refused to recognize the new state, Japan withdrew from the League. In Germany, economic conditions like those in the United States enabled confrontations between fascist and communist factions. German business leaders supported the fascists in exchange for Hitler's promise not to nationalize their assets, compelling Hindenburg's government to accept Hitler as Chancellor in January 1933. Hitler's Nazi coalition won a majority of seats in the German Reichstag (Congress) within days of FDR's inauguration. The Reichstag immediately gave Hitler all the power he needed to defy the restrictions placed on Germany's military by the Versailles Treaty and begin the Nazi's state-sponsored persecution of the Jewish people.

Under Hitler, Germany proceeded to rebuild its military, in violation of the Versailles Treaty. Italy invaded Ethiopia in October of 1935. In July of 1936, the Spanish Civil War began with a military coup. The following summer, Japan continued its aggression in Asia by invading the portion of China not already under its control. At the end of 1937, Japanese planes sank an American gunboat near Nanking, killing three Americans. The Japanese claimed the attack was an accident, apologized and paid reparations. In 1938, Hitler used his rearmed military to seize

Austria. As he ramped up his rhetoric regarding the need to protect ethnic Germans in Czechoslovakia, Britain and France made a desperate, last-ditch effort with the Munich Accord to preserve peace through appeasement, giving Germany the Czech territory known as the Sudetenland. In March of 1939, however, Germany seized all of Czechoslovakia. Finally, when Germany invaded Poland in September of that year, treaty obligations forced France and Britain to declare war on Germany, marking what historians generally consider the start of the Second World War.

The widespread belief that America could avoid foreign wars through isolationism and neutrality constrained FDR's response to the events leading up to World War II. Vocal isolationist and pacifist elements dominated the United States Congress. In 1928, U.S. Secretary of State Frank Kellogg had a leading role in crafting a treaty wherein nearly every country in the world pledged not to go to war to resolve international disputes. The treaty had no provisions for enforcing the pledge. With only one dissenting vote, the U.S. Senate quickly ratified the so-called Kellogg-Briand Treaty. In contrast, FDR's efforts to get the United States to join the World Court in January of 1935 failed when five Democrats joined thirty-one Republicans to reject the measure in the Senate. Later in 1935, college students boycotted classes in a peace strike that reflected the sentiments of the Kellogg-Briand Treaty. In August of that year, Congress passed the first of four Neutrality Acts, prohibiting shipments of "arms, ammunition, or implements of war" to any country involved in a war. In 1938, Congressman Louis Ludlow proposed a constitutional amendment requiring a popular vote before any declaration of war.

Despite the political strength of the isolationists, FDR was successful in preparing the American people for the possibility of war, gaining additional funding to prepare the United States military for war, and providing essential moral and material support for America's allies. In 1938, he publicly opposed the Ludlow amendment and sent diplomatic messages to Germany and Italy encouraging them to use diplomacy to resolve international disputes. Then, during his State of the Union address in January of 1939, FDR explained why international aggression threatened American democracy. He asked for a significant increase in defense funding, and he asked for legislation to prevent aggressor nations from benefiting from American neutrality laws. In response to Germany's continued aggression during 1939, Roosevelt used administrative measures that did not require congressional approval to punish Germany.

Roosevelt relentlessly prodded Congress while using radio to effectively communicate his concerns to the American people. After war broke out between the major European powers, he called for a special session of Congress to modify the neutrality laws that they had failed to address previously. In a radio address to the American people, he asserted that he was as determined as ever to keep America out of the war while explaining to the American people why it was necessary to lift the arms embargo imposed by the neutrality law. In 1940, FDR again asked for increased defense spending and successfully lobbied Congress to pass the first peacetime draft legislation in American history. Following the rapid Nazi conquest of France in June of that year, he worked directly with Winston Churchill to get Britain the support they needed to continue to fight. In another radio address that December, he explained why building America's defenses and becoming the "arsenal of democracy" was the best way to keep America safe. Then, at his State of the Union address just one week later, he outlined four freedoms that America sought to achieve by providing arms to countries fighting aggression: freedom of expression, freedom of religion, freedom from want, and freedom from fear. FDR succeeded in getting the Lend-Lease Act through Congress in March of 1941, providing Britain with fifty much-needed destroyers in exchange for leasing rights to a large number of strategic bases throughout the British empire. By this time, public opinion favored his policy to arm countries fighting aggression. American industry ramped up, and the United States provided support to Britain, the Soviet Union, and China to counter the aggression of Germany, Italy and Japan. When the Japanese attacked Pearl Harbor on December 7, 1941, the preparatory actions FDR had taken during the preceding four years enabled America to respond more rapidly and ultimately win the war.

FDR addressed a joint session of Congress on December 8, 1941, and asked that Congress declare war on Japan. He spoke for only a few minutes, and both the Senate and the House of Representatives approved the war resolution in less than an hour. The following evening, Roosevelt spoke to the American people in a radio address. He made the case that the Japanese attack on the United States was part of the pattern of aggression that included the actions of Germany, Italy and Japan over the past ten years. He said that America would have to defeat all of the aggressor nations to protect itself, and that it would be a long, hard fight. On December 11, 1941, Germany and Italy declared war on the United States. The United States Congress immediately responded in kind.

For the remainder of his time as president, FDR harnessed and directed the will of the American people, in coordination with our allies, to not only win the war but also to shape the world that would emerge after the war. In preparation for his radio address in February, 1942, for example, he asked the American people to listen with a map of the world in front of them, so they could better understand where American soldiers would have to fight. Conferences throughout the war with leaders of allied nations provided a venue to resolve differences over strategic priorities. Roosevelt also used these events effectively to achieve consensus on a post-war organization he called the united nations, as well as on the general nature of post-war arrangements to rebuild economies and foster a stable peace.

FDR ranks among the very best of American presidents for good reason. During his time in office, Roosevelt guided America to overcome two existential crises: the Great Depression and World War II. He won each of his four general elections with an overwhelming number of electoral votes: 472 to 59 in 1932, 523 to 8 in 1936, 449 to 82 in 1940, and 423 to 99 in 1944. Roosevelt, the heir of a wealthy and prominent New York family, was a political progressive who fought for a more equitable distribution of the benefits of American society. His New Deal policies provided relief for Americans suffering from hunger and homelessness during the Great Depression while establishing institutional guardrails to prevent similar economic meltdowns in the future. His inspiring leadership ensured the defeat of aggression in World War II and made possible a more stable peace. Franklin Delano Roosevelt died on April 12, 1945, eighty-three days into his fourth term.

CHAPTER 4

Why The Worst Are The Worst

People often say one can learn more from failures than from successes. If this is so, then we should pay special attention to the presidents who most consistently rank at the bottom of the forty-two men in our data set. Franklin Pierce, James Buchanan, Andrew Johnson, and Warren Harding rank in the bottom five presidents in all four surveys used for this study. There are clearly identifiable failures in their presidencies, and we can contrast these failures with the successes noted in the last chapter. In the order in which they served as president, this chapter examines the historical context, the significant events, and the legacy of their presidencies.

These presidents rank poorly for a number of reasons. The policies of Pierce and Buchanan divided Americans of their day and failed to meet the challenge of avoiding civil war. Buchanan tampered with the Supreme Court to change the scope of the Dred Scott decision. Johnson failed to keep his oath to "preserve, protect and defend the Constitution" and allowed legal manipulations to perpetuate racial violence and injustice against African-Americans. Both he and Harding may be said to have missed the significant opportunity afforded them at their moment in history: they both used their presidency to try to restore something from the past when the moment called for visionary leadership towards a better future. The Buchanan and Harding administrations were tainted with corruption. The failures of these men--our worst presidents--are stark indicators of what we should not choose in the next presidential election: candidates who divide, candidates who encourage or tolerate violence, candidates tainted with corruption, and anyone who has inappropriately interfered with the proper function of constitutional mechanisms to secure their preferred outcome.

Franklin Pierce: The Fourteenth President (1853-1857)

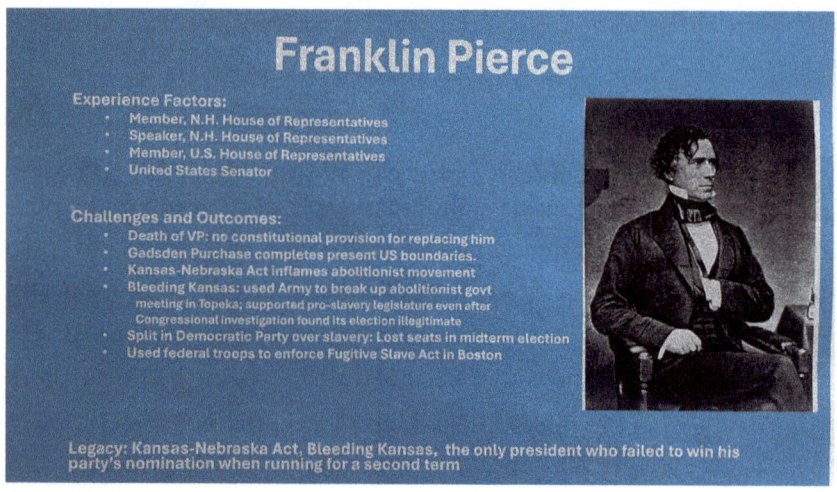

Historical Context: 1787-1860

Without compromises to allow the continuation of slavery, it is unlikely that there could have been a Constitution or a unified country formed from the original thirteen states. Some sources estimate that between seventeen and twenty-five of the delegates to the constitutional convention owned slaves. George Washington was a slave owner for his entire life, having inherited his first slaves upon the death of his father when he was eleven.

Washington became increasingly uncomfortable with the practice of slavery during his life. In his will, he freed some slaves immediately upon his death while making provisions for others to be freed upon the death of his wife. In some of his personal letters and statements, he stated that he wished slavery could be

ended, but that he thought the only proper way to bring about the end of slavery was through legislation.

The compromises over slavery in the Constitution essentially gave slave states extra power in Congress based on their slave population and protected the slave trade from congressional prohibition for a specified period. Since representation and power in Congress is based on statehood and population, each addition of territory after 1789 was a potential change to the congressional balance of power. Senators and Representatives from slave states, therefore, sought to make slavery legal in new territories and states. Those representing free states sought to prevent the spread of slavery as new territory was added.

In the summer of 1787, while the delegates in Philadelphia were still working on the Constitution, the Congress passed the Northwest Ordinance banning slavery in the region that would eventually become the states of Illinois, Indiana, Michigan, Ohio, Wisconsin and Minnesota. After that, the United States expanded again through the Louisiana Purchase of 1803, which added territory west of the Mississippi River that was claimed by the French. The Missouri Compromise of 1820 established a line to limit the spread of slavery in this area. Slavery was to be prohibited north of the line and allowed south of it.

In 1821, the United States acquired Florida and the Oregon Territory from Spain. Florida did not become a state, however, until 1845. On March 3 of that year, Congress passed the Iowa-Florida Act. Under this legislation, Florida became a slave state and Iowa came in as a free state, preserving the balance of power between pro-slavery and anti-slavery forces in Congress.

Texas won its independence from Mexico in 1836. Many Texans wanted to join the United States right away. Since there was slavery in Texas, however, admitting it as another slave state was controversial. Congress voted to annex Texas and make it a state on December 29, 1845.

After Texas became part of the United States, a dispute over the border between Texas and Mexico led to the Mexican-American War (1846-48). The United States invaded Mexico and captured Mexico City. Under the treaty that ended the war, the United States paid Mexico $15 million for territory that included California, Arizona, New Mexico, and parts of Utah, Nevada and Colorado. The addition of all this territory reignited the political crisis over the status of slavery in the United States.

Henry Clay, the Whig senator who had crafted the Missouri Compromise thirty years earlier, put forward a collection of legislative measures that came to be known as the Compromise of 1850. This package of legislation allowed California statehood as a free state, provided that the status of slavery in the Utah Territory would be decided by vote (popular sovereignty), and reinforced the legal obligation of all citizens to return escaped slaves to their masters. It also established the New Mexico Territory with no restriction on slavery there. Texas gave up its claims to these western territories in exchange for the federal government assuming responsibility for the public debt of the former Republic of Texas.

While widely credited with forestalling civil war, the Compromise of 1850 revealed serious fault lines within both the Whig Party and the Democratic Party. Clay's anti-slavery Whig colleague Henry Seward spoke against the Compromise, saying there could be no compromise with slavery and citing a power higher than the Constitution. Pro-slave Democratic Senator John C. Calhoun's statement expressed his opposition to the Compromise while stating forcefully that slavery must not be restricted from spreading to the territories. So, while the Compromise of 1850 may have delayed civil war, it also made clear that there were strong feelings on both sides of the slavery issue that would not be easily reconciled. Indeed, as the 1850s progressed, some congressional debates over slavery broke down into fist fights and confrontations with drawn guns. In the spring of 1852, Harriet Beecher Stowe published *Uncle Tom's Cabin*. Her work popularized the anti-slavery cause and moved the population in northern states to greater sympathy for those enslaved in the south. Later that year, a divided Whig party lost the presidential election to Democrat Franklin Pierce.

The Presidency of Franklin Pierce

Franklin Pierce ranks among the four worst presidents of the United States in all four surveys used in the analysis on which this book is based. Pierce served as the fourteenth president from 1853 to 1857. Although he believed slavery was morally wrong, he also believed the federal government did not have the right to make slavery illegal in a state or territory. He believed that the actions of abolitionists to oppose slavery were more of a threat to the unity of the United States than slavery itself. By favoring pro-slavery interests, Pierce abandoned the process and precedent of legislative compromise and created conditions where both sides felt they had to solve the slavery question through violence.

Southern senators would not allow the organization of land in the Louisiana Territory because the Missouri Compromise of 1820 made slavery illegal in this area. Other legislators wanted the land organized into territories to support construction of the transcontinental railroad. Congress passed the Kansas-Nebraska Act, which repealed the Missouri Compromise, created territories of Kansas and Nebraska, and left the question of slavery up to a vote by the people living in the territory. Pierce signed the Kansas-Nebraska Act into law on May 30, 1854, setting off a rush by both pro and anti-slavery factions to control the status of slavery in Kansas.

The competition for Kansas immediately turned violent. So much violence took place by both pro and anti-slavery partisans that the episode has become known as Bleeding Kansas. Some of the incidents commonly cited are the murder of five pro-slavery men by abolitionist John Brown and the burning of the city of Lawrence by pro-slavery forces. Pierce attempted to stop the violence by appointing a military governor for the Kansas Territory, but this had only limited success.

After anti-slavery legislators passed an anti-slavery constitution (Topeka Constitution, 1856), the pro-slavery faction brought in thousands of men from Missouri to swing the referendum on slavery in their favor, electing a pro-slavery legislature in Lecompton and enacting the pro-slavery Lecompton Constitution (1857). Pierce recognized the pro-slavery legislature, maintaining this position even after a congressional investigation revealed that the voting was not legitimate because of the large number of Missouri men who had voted. He condemned the anti-slavery Topeka Constitution even though it was the first constitution sent to Congress by Kansas legislators. When the anti-slavery faction established a shadow government in Topeka, Pierce used federal troops to prevent them from meeting.

The unpopularity of the Kansas-Nebraska Act, along with Pierce's use of federal troops both to support the pro-slavery faction in Kansas and to enforce the Fugitive Slave Act elsewhere, drew a strong anti-slavery reaction at the polls for the midterm election in 1854. Pierce himself made history in 1856 by becoming the first sitting president to seek and be denied the nomination of his party for a second-term presidential election. Whatever Pierce believed regarding the possibility that popular sovereignty in Kansas would settle the issue of slavery, he was clearly wrong. His actions in supporting the pro-slavery factions were divisive, invited violence, and put the country on the road to civil war.

What could Pierce have done differently? If he had stuck by the historical precedent of the Missouri Compromise and vetoed the Kansas-Nebraska Act, it is at least possible that the financial forces backing the transcontinental railroad could have eventually overcome the pro-slavery senators' objections, allowing Kansas to enter the Union with the Missouri Compromise intact. It is at least possible that the Bleeding Kansas episode could have been avoided. Although we can never know if that would have worked, it does seem clear that, by putting the full weight of the federal government in support of the pro-slavery side in the Kansas-Nebraska saga, Pierce failed to successfully navigate the defining crisis of his presidency.

James Buchanan: The Fifteenth President (1857-1861)

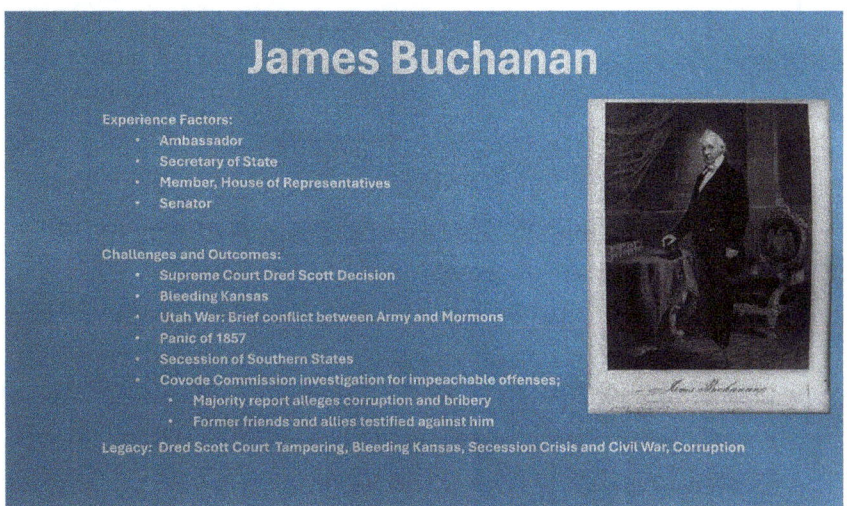

Historical Context: 1854-1860

The passage of the Kansas-Nebraska Act was a shock to many in the north, including a young Whig lawyer named Abraham Lincoln. Lincoln believed the assertion in the Declaration of Independence, that all are created equal, applied to slaves as well as to white men. He believed that the founding fathers had only allowed slavery to persist out of necessity: because it was already deeply embedded in the economies of many states and could not be removed immediately. He believed that the founders had intended slavery to be limited to the states where it existed in 1789, that they intended the practice of slavery to eventually die out, and that the Missouri Compromise reinforced these sentiments.

When the Kansas-Nebraska Act passed, Lincoln was roused to act because he came to see that pro-slavery forces did not share the vision he had ascribed to the founders for the eventual extinction of slavery. Just a few months later, on October 4, he gave his first great anti-slavery speech in rebuttal to Senator Douglas at the Illinois State Fair. He and Douglas would go on to a series of seven debates over the issue of slavery in 1858 when both men competed for Douglas' Senate seat.

Lincoln was not alone in his strong opposition to the Kansas-Nebraska Act: across the north there were mass protests and thousands signed resolutions opposing the Act. The Whig Party essentially died, and a new anti-slavery Republican Party took root in 1854. Lincoln took a leadership role in the Illinois Republican Party, a step that would eventually result in his election as our sixteenth president in 1860.

But in the election of 1856, the Whigs were in the process of disbanding. Many former Whigs joined the new Republican Party. A number of prominent leaders took their names out of consideration for the Republican presidential nomination. The Republicans nominated John C. Fremont, a former United States Senator from California, as their presidential candidate. The Democrats, after denying their incumbent Pierce the nomination, put forward James Buchanan as their candidate. Buchanan won the election, and was sworn in as the fifteenth President of the United States on March 4, 1857.

The Presidency of James Buchanan

James Buchanan ranks as the worst president in three of the four surveys used in the analysis that underlies this book. He ranks as the second-worst president in the fourth survey. Buchanan served as the fifteenth president from 1857 to 1861. Like Pierce, he believed both that slavery was morally wrong, that the federal government could not restrict slavery in states or territories, and that anti-slavery factions were the greatest threat to the survival of the United States. He is widely considered the worst president in the history of the United States not only because he failed to stop the Civil War, but because he undermined constitutional checks and balances by inappropriately influencing the Supreme Court's decision in *Dred Scott v. Sandford*, he continued the failed policies of Franklin Pierce that allowed violence over slavery to escalate, and he presided over an administration that used corrupt means to achieve its ends.

Between his election in November of 1856 and his inauguration (March 4, 1857), Buchanan inappropriately influenced the outcome of a Supreme Court case on slavery. Dred Scott was a slave who had sued for his freedom in a lower court. The case went through the appeals process over several years and was tried before the Supreme Court at the beginning of 1856, several months prior to the election. The Court's decision was tending toward a narrow ruling against Scott that would have minimal wider application with regard to the status of slavery in various states and territories. But Buchanan spoke with one of the Justices, who suggested that the only way a broader ruling was possible would be if Buchanan could get a northern Justice to side with the southern majority on the Court. Buchanan acted on this information. At his urging, Justice Grier, a fellow Pennsylvanian, joined the majority with a short, one-paragraph affirmation of the more detailed arguments of another Justice. The Court ruled 7-2 against Scott. With the strong majority Buchanan had inappropriately secured, the Court ruled broadly that Congress did not have the constitutional authority to restrict slavery from any state or territory. There were nearly immediate allegations of impropriety regarding the ruling and Buchanan's involvement in shaping it. Historians consider the angry backlash to the Court's ruling in *Dred Scott v. Sandford* a significant factor accelerating the country's descent into civil war (Baker 113).

Buchanan also continued to support the failed, pro-slavery stance of Franklin Pierce with regard to the process of slavery in Kansas. The first state constitution to come out of the state was anti-slavery, and pro-slavery forces wrote a second constitution, called the Lecompton Constitution, to take its place. The Lecompton Constitution was approved in a rigged election in December of 1857 before being strongly rejected by voters in January of 1858. Nevertheless, Buchanan endorsed the Lecompton Constitution and sent it to Congress on February 2, 1858. The Senate approved Kansas for statehood as a slave state. The House of Representatives voted against statehood for Kansas in a fiery debate that allegedly included a fistfight. It would be another three years before Congress would admit Kansas as a free state under the Wyandotte Constitution on January 29, 1861.

Buchanan's heavy-handed use of federal power to support pro-slavery forces in Kansas contributed to additional violence as the nation sought a solution to the slavery issue. From April to June of 1858, in the wake of the Senate action in favor of making Kansas a slave state, there were several clashes between anti-slavery partisans and federal troops in the southeastern part of the state. In October of 1859, the violence over slavery spilled outside of Kansas when John Brown led a raid on the federal armory at Harper's Ferry, Virginia, hoping to start a slave revolt. Brown was arrested and hanged.

Buchanan and his administration are also considered among the most corrupt in American history. Jean Baker's biography of Buchanan states that many in government believed Buchanan and his inner circle "had reached unacceptable levels in terms of the use of public authority and funds for private and party profit"(Baker 113). The majority report of the United States House Select Committee To Investigate Alleged Corruptions in Government cited evidence of corruption. Some allegations include Buchanan attempting to bribe Members of Congress to buy votes supporting Kansas statehood under the Lecompton Constitution, as well as awarding contracts to political supporters without following normal competitive processes and using government money and property as bribes. Buchanan called the congressional investigation an "inquisition", but several of his former allies and friends testified against him. While the committee ultimately did not vote to impeach Buchanan, it presented significant evidence of inappropriate conduct (Baker 113-14).

Andrew Johnson: The Seventeenth President (1865-1869)

Historical Context: 1861-1868

Reconstruction refers to the period near the end of the Civil War when the federal government was attempting to end slavery, integrate former slaves into society as citizens, and bring the secessionist southern states back into the Union. While there are various dates used to frame this period, for our purposes it is useful to mark it from the date of the Emancipation Proclamation (January 1, 1863) until the date the last federal troops were withdrawn from occupying the south in 1877. Understanding Reconstruction is essential to understanding the failure of Andrew Johnson's presidency.

There were a number of distinct factions that contributed to the difficulty of Reconstruction. Copperheads, or anti-war Democrats, favored an immediate end to the fighting without regard for any change in the institution of slavery. War Democrats were members of the Democratic Party who rejected secession and supported the war and the restoration of the Union. Radicals were Republicans who favored abolition of slavery, full and immediate citizenship for former slaves, and harsh punishment for those who participated in the rebellion of the southern states. Conservative Republicans favored compensation for emancipating the slaves, and were more lenient in allowing those who had supported the rebellion to regain voting rights.

In *Team of Rivals*, her classic biography of President Lincoln, Doris Kearns Goodwin reports that Lincoln considered the problem of Reconstruction to be "the greatest question ever presented to practical statesmanship"(588). In his 1863 State of the Union address, he proposed an original approach that seemed to satisfy both the conservative and radical elements of the Republican Party. As a starting point, his proposal was to insist that swearing allegiance to the Union and accepting emancipation were essential before any citizen of the rebel states would be pardoned. At the same time, he resisted those who wished an extremely punitive approach to reconstruction. With some exceptions for the most senior leaders, he was willing to offer full pardons to those in the confederate states who met his essential conditions. Further, he proposed that when the number of men in a state to meet his conditions reached ten percent of the votes cast in the 1860 election, that state could re-establish a government recognized by the United States, with the names and boundaries of the state unchanged. Finally, he noted that he would consider modifications to his proposal as the process of reconstruction moved forward. His intent was to encourage the southern states to rejoin the Union sooner rather than later, perhaps bringing the war to a speedier conclusion. Only four months after delivering this address, and less than a week after Lee surrendered to Grant at Appomattox, Lincoln was assassinated, leaving the challenge of reconstruction to his vice president, Andrew Johnson.

Reconstruction Timeline

Event	Date
Emancipation Proclamation	January 1, 1863
Lincoln Re-elected	November 8, 1864
State of the Union Address	December 6, 1864
Lee surrenders to Grant	April 9, 1865
Lincoln Assassinated	April 15, 1865
XVIII Amendment ends Slavery	December 6, 1865
Civil Rights Act of 1866 Passed over Johnson's Veto	April 9, 1866
Andrew Johnson Impeached	February 24, 1868
XIV Amendment (Equal Protection of Law)	July 9, 1868
End of Reconstruction	1877

Under the control of Republicans who favored an intensive Reconstruction, Congress passed a number of measures intended to assure the rights of citizenship to former slaves. The Thirteenth Amendment, approved by Congress on January 31, 1865, ended slavery; it officially became part of the Constitution when Georgia ratified it on December 6th, 1865. On March 3, 1865, Congress also established a government agency--the Freedman's Bureau--to help former slaves transition to freedom and economic independence. The Civil Rights Act of 1866 guaranteed the rights of citizenship to all persons. This law was supposed to guarantee the rights of citizenship to former slaves and people of African descent; it was enacted into law on April 9, 1866. Congress passed the Fourteenth Amendment on January 8, 1866. This amendment reversed the ruling of *Dred Scott v. Sandford* by extending the rights of citizenship to all persons born or naturalized in the United States and guaranteeing equal protection of the laws to all people in our country (regardless of citizenship). It became part of the Constitution when South Carolina ratified it on July 9, 1868. The Fifteenth Amendment prohibits the states or the federal government from restricting the right to vote based on race, color or previous condition of servitude. It became part of the Constitution when Iowa ratified it on February 3, 1870. Three enforcement acts were passed in 1870 and 1871 to allow for the use of the Army to enforce the rights guaranteed under the new amendments, to provide for federal oversight of elections within a state, and to allow for federal prosecution of those denying voting rights or equal protection of the law to former slaves.

In spite of these legislative efforts at the federal level, deeply ingrained racism persisted and allowed local authorities to deny equal rights to former slaves. Black Codes and Jim Crow laws took root. The use of federal power met with some temporary success, but the end of Reconstruction ushered in an extended period of racial injustice.

The Presidency of Andrew Johnson

Andrew Johnson ranks among the four worst presidents of the United States in all four surveys used in the analysis on which this book is based. Johnson served as the governor of Tennessee from 1853 to 1857, and as a United States Senator from 1857 to 1862. He was a "war Democrat" who opposed secession. He supported fighting the war to restore the Union. He also was the only sitting senator from a seceding state who did not resign from his Senate post. President Lincoln made him the military governor of Tennessee in 1862.

The Republican Party, temporarily re-branded as the National Union Party to attract the support of war Democrats and Unionists, chose Johnson to be the vice president on Lincoln's ticket at their convention in Baltimore in June of 1864. Lincoln expressed no preference among the candidates for vice president, which also included his first-term vice president Hannibal Hamlin (Republican) and former New York senator Daniel Dickinson (Democrat). According to Doris Kearns Goodwin's excellent summary in *Team of Rivals*, Johnson was favored by the convention delegates because he broadened the appeal of Lincoln's ticket to war Democrats and he was from a state that was not already represented in Lincoln's cabinet (624-26).

Johnson was a slave owner and a white supremacist. Although Tennessee was one of the states not covered by Lincoln's Emancipation Proclamation, Johnson freed his slaves in 1863. He ordered the mass emancipation of all slaves in Tennessee in 1864. Although he supported ending slavery, he opposed efforts to protect former slaves and to provide them the rights of citizenship.

Johnson took the oath of office and became president a few hours after President Lincoln's death on April 15, 1865. He served the remainder of Lincoln's second term and lost the election of 1868 to Ulysses S. Grant. Johnson ranks as one of our worst presidents because he failed to seize the opportunity presented by Lincoln's presidency and the Union victory in the Civil War, he failed to meet the challenge of Reconstruction, and he enabled white supremacy in the former confederate states through his opposition to legislative and constitutional provisions protecting the rights of former slaves.

In conjunction with his 1863 State of the Union Address to Congress, President Lincoln issued a *Proclamation of Amnesty and Reconstruction*. In his remarks to Congress, Lincoln outlined his reasoning for reconstructing the governments of seceded states, but he also stated that "a revived State government, constructed in whole or in preponderating part from the very element against whose hostility and violence it [the state] is to be protected, is simply absurd." He expressed his firm commitment to the emancipation of all slaves freed under the Emancipation Proclamation. Specifically, he stated "To now abandon them [the laws and proclamations with regard to slavery] would be not only to relinquish a lever of power, but would also be a cruel and astounding breach of faith." He indicated his intent to support "any reasonable temporary State arrangement for the freed people" while asserting that his plans would not surrender any "power of the National Executive to prevent an abuse..." (Lincoln "1863..."). According to Doris Kearns Goodwin's summary in *Team of Rivals*, Lincoln's assurances that he would not allow reconstruction to simply re-establish the confederate states under a different guise and that he would use executive power to protect the freed slaves were essential in gaining congressional support for his plan (588-89). Lincoln's enactment of the first Freedman's Bureau bill on March 3, 1865, is further evidence of his intent to impose a Reconstruction with real protections for former slaves.

The newly elected 39th Congress was out of session when President Lincoln was assassinated. Upon taking the oath of office, President Johnson sought to complete Reconstruction with presidential authorities before Congress came back into session in December. To accomplish this, he issued a series of presidential directives. Although these directives were consistent with the outlines of the plan Lincoln announced at the end of 1863, Johnson's rushed implementation allowed the formation of the type of state governments that Lincoln told Congress he would not support: governments based predominantly on the governments of the confederacy. At the time Johnson declared the Union restored, some of the former confederate state governments had failed to meet the basic requirements in Johnson's own directives. For instance, neither Texas nor Mississippi had ratified the Thirteenth Amendment abolishing slavery. Nonetheless, Johnson held that these states could fully participate in the government, including sending representatives to the United States Congress.

When Congress reconvened on December 4th, 1865, Congressional leaders refused to recognize representatives sent from the former confederate states. They convened a Joint Committee on Reconstruction which investigated the conditions in the states that had seceded from the Union. The Report of the Joint Committee on Reconstruction, citing the Constitution of the United States, held that only Congress had the authority to decide on the qualifications of its members. With regard to President Johnson's attempt to restore the congressional representation of the seceded states, the report states that "the evidence upon which the President seemed to have based his suggestions was incomplete and unsatisfactory"("Report of the Joint Committee..."). Congress then proceeded to establish its own plan for Reconstruction and to pass a number of measures to guarantee and protect the rights of the freed slaves.

Congress passed the Civil Rights Act of 1866, and President Johnson vetoed it. Congress overrode the veto on April 9th, thereby enacting it. This was the first time Congress overrode a presidential veto on major legislation. Johnson vetoed a bill to extend the Freedman's Bureau in July of 1866, and Congress overrode that veto as well. This pattern continued as Congress enacted a series of Reconstruction Acts that superimposed five military governorships over the former rebel states and established more rigorous requirements for those states to normalize their relationship to the federal government. In advance of the 1866 midterm elections, President Johnson went on a public speaking tour in an unsuccessful attempt to undermine congressional authority on Reconstruction with a series of inflammatory and divisive speeches. Election results strongly reinforced the efforts of Congress, effectively neutering Johnson for the remainder of his presidency.

The following year, Congress enacted the Tenure of Office Act over the president's veto, making it illegal for the president to fire any executive officer appointed with the advice and consent of the Senate without the approval of the Senate. The purpose of this law was to prevent President Johnson from replacing Lincoln's Secretary of War with someone less willing to support congressional Reconstruction initiatives. When the President attempted to replace Secretary Stanton anyway, Congress impeached him. The impeachment alleged eleven offenses, including a charge related to his divisive speeches in advance of the previous year's election. In the trial before the Senate, Johnson was acquitted by one vote.

It is impossible to know what could have happened if Johnson had pursued a Reconstruction policy more consistent with the course Lincoln had set. President Lincoln, in his guidance to the general in charge of occupied Louisiana, had expressed the hope for "some practical system by which the two races could gradually live themselves out of their old relation to each other..."("The Civil War..."). We know only that, with Lincoln's assassination, Johnson pursued a Reconstruction based on preserving white supremacy. Although congressional Reconstruction mitigated Johnson's policies, the conflict and division that characterized his presidency squandered the opportunity for a united federal government to impose a coherent plan that would foster racial justice and harmony. As a result, it would be another hundred years before a president could muster the political will to confront the ingrained racism that is the legacy of slavery in America.

Warren Harding: The Twenty-ninth President (1921-1923)

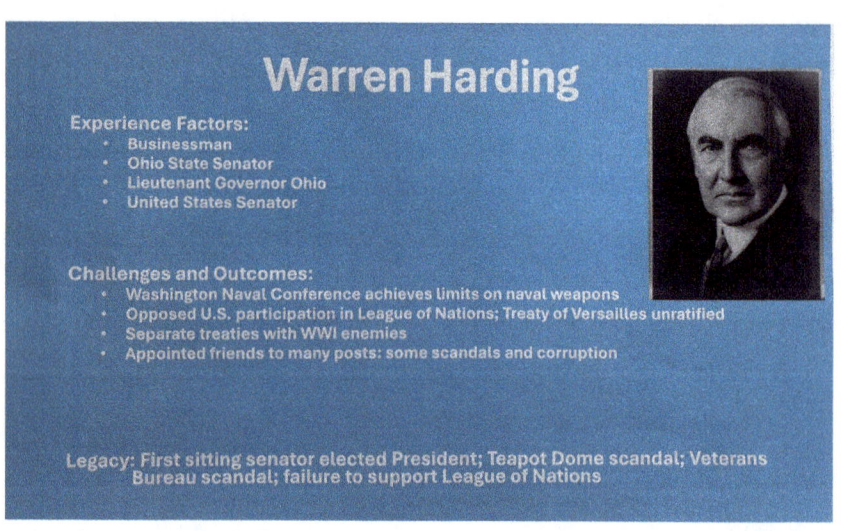

Historical Context: 1787-1935

Some of the basic operations of our federal government are different today than they were in the past. Understanding these changes and when they came about is important: the presidents discussed in this book operated under different circumstances with respect to Congress and their transition from election to inauguration. Specifically, the Seventeenth Amendment changed the Constitution to provide for direct elections for United States Senators (from having senators elected by state legislatures), and the Twentieth Amendment provided for specific dates in January of the year following an election for the seating of a new Congress and the end-of-term for the president and vice president.

The Seventeenth Amendment to the United States Constitution was ratified on April 8, 1913. This amendment provided for the direct election of senators by the people in each state. Originally, senators were chosen by the state legislatures for terms of six years. The Constitution provided for dividing the Senate into three classes so that only one-third of the Senate is subject to election in any given general election. By the late 1800s, divided legislatures in some states were unable to agree on a senator, leaving vacancies for extended times. By the time the Seventeenth Amendment was introduced, many states had evolved to a system where people voted for their desired senator in a state primary, and candidates for the legislature pledged to honor the result of the primary. The general election of 1914 was the first time all senators of the class subject to election were chosen by direct vote.

The Twentieth Amendment to the United States Constitution was ratified January 23, 1933. This amendment provided that that terms of the president and vice president would end on January 20 of the year following an election of a new president. This also had the effect of moving up the inauguration of the newly elected president from the first week in March to the end of January, reducing the length of the so-called lame duck period between and election and the inauguration. It also changed the starting date for new sessions of Congress from the first Monday in December following an election to January 3 or a date appointed by law.

The Presidency of Warren Harding

Warren Harding ranks among the four worst presidents of the United States in three of the four surveys used in the analysis on which this book is based. He is somewhat of an outlier in this regard, as he was well-liked by his political contemporaries and enjoyed great popularity as president until his death by heart attack on August 2, 1923. He did some really good things as president, including enacting the Sheppard-Towner Act to provide federal funding for maternity care in rural America (reducing infant mortality) and advocating for the Dyer Anti-Lynching Bill (which was blocked by filibuster in the Senate). While the most obvious reason for his ranking among our worst presidents are the numerous scandals within his administration revealed after his death, his platform of "return to normalcy" arguably missed an opportunity in U.S. foreign policy to avoid much of the tragedy of the next thirty years for both America as well as the rest of the world.

Harding's path to the White House began with ownership of his hometown newspaper, extended through a number of Ohio state political offices, and was marked by an extraordinary ability to navigate political issues without alienating his contemporaries. He served in the Ohio State Senate and two years as Lieutenant Governor, earning a reputation as someone who could negotiate difficult compromise solutions. In 1914, he was elected in the first class of senators elected by popular vote under the Seventeenth Amendment. He was a long-shot candidate for the Republican presidential nomination in 1920, and won the nomination as a compromise when the conference deadlocked and was unable to decide between the leading contenders. Campaigning on the non-controversial "return to normalcy" platform, Harding won in a landslide over Democrat James Cox.

The widespread corruption within the Harding administration involved a number of the friends and political associates whom he appointed to his cabinet. This group included former Senate colleague Albert Fall, Charles Forbes, Ohio political colleague Harry Daugherty, Daugherty's friend Jess Smith, and former Delaware congressman Thomas W. Miller. Albert Fall, as Secretary of the Interior, was later convicted for taking bribes in exchange for underselling oil leases in the infamous Teapot Dome scandal. He served time in prison for crimes committed as Secretary of the Interior. Harding appointed Forbes as the first Head of the Veterans Bureau, and he was later found guilty of making over $200 million off of corrupt activities in this office. Jess Smith was accused of influence peddling and corruption, including taking payoffs from alcohol bootleggers. He also helped Miller, whom Harding had appointed as Alien Property Custodian, with a scheme involving a $500,000 bribe for releasing a German-owned company to American owners. Smith was found shot in the head with a gun by his side, allegedly a suicide. Miller was convicted and served time in prison for the Alien Property scheme. Daugherty was investigated for involvement with all of these schemes, but was never convicted. Although Harding was not implicated in any of these schemes, the scale of corruption in his administration and the fact that he was personally close with this group, frequently playing cards with them in the White House, is certainly cause for marking Harding as failing in his constitutional duty to "take Care that the Laws be faithfully executed"(The Constitution...).

At another level, the premise of Harding's platform of "return to normalcy" reflected a profound misunderstanding of the role America had assumed in the world by 1920. In 1914, the United States had been the world's largest debtor nation, with foreign ownership of United States assets on the order of $3 billion. By 1920, the United States had become the world's largest creditor. The war had devastated the labor pool, agriculture, industry and infrastructure of the European countries. These countries owed the United States something on the order of $11 billion. Given this reality, the idea of a return to a pre-war normalcy was at least implausible.

Abandoning Wilson's efforts to build a stable post-war community of nations denied the new reality facing America. As the president-elect, with Wilson stricken by a stroke and unable to continue to articulate the necessary support for the Treaty of Versailles, it was incumbent on Harding to take a leadership role in a position that would have undoubtedly been unpopular with his party.

Certainly there were legitimate reasons for the Senate to want to revise the Treaty of Versailles. Article X in particular, requiring all nations to fight to oppose aggression, probably was a step too far. But simply failing to ratify the treaty rather than modify it was a failure. It forced the United States to negotiate its own separate treaties with the belligerents, which took several years. Moreover, it denied America the leadership opportunity that it had as a result of its economic and military victory in the World War. Without the participation of the world's largest creditor, the League of Nations was doomed from the start.

The decade between the end of World War I and the Great Depression included two significant treaties that aimed at reducing armaments and discouraging war as a tool for resolving their differences. The Washington Naval Treaty of 1922 was a significant arms control achievement that committed Great Britain, the United States, France, Italy and Japan to significant reductions in warships. The Kellogg-Briand Pact of 1928 committed nearly all nations to deny war as a means to resolve disagreements. It is difficult not to imagine what could have been had the United States embraced a leadership role in the League of Nations at the beginning of Harding's presidency. Without the looming threat of atomic bombs that confronted the world in 1945, a League of Nations with American leadership in 1920 might well have avoided the tragedy of the Second World War. One cannot help but fault Harding for trading this possibility for the politically expedient but practically impossible "return to normalcy."

CHAPTER 5

Five Legacy Addresses

President Abraham Lincoln
The Gettysburg Address
November 19, 1863

Four score and seven years ago, our fathers brought forth upon this continent, a new nation, conceived in Liberty, and dedicated to the proposition that all men are created equal.

Now we are engaged in a great civil war, testing whether that nation, or any nation so conceived, and so dedicated, can long endure. We are met on a great battle-field of that war. We have come to dedicate a portion of that field, as a final resting place for those who here gave their lives, that that nation might live. It is altogether fitting and proper that we should do this.

But, in a larger sense, we can not dedicate--we can not consecrate--we can not hallow--this ground. The brave men, living and dead, who struggled here, have consecrated it, far above our poor power to add or detract. The world will little note, nor long remember, what we say here, but it can never forget what they did here. It is for us, the living, rather, to be dedicated here to the unfinished work which they who fought here, have, thus far, so nobly advanced. It is rather for us to be here dedicated to the great task remaining before us--that from these honored dead we take increased devotion to that cause for which they here gave the last full measure of devotion--that we here highly resolve that these dead shall not have died in vain--that this nation, under God, shall have a new birth of freedom--and that, government of the people, by the people, for the people, shall not perish from the earth.

President Abraham Lincoln
The Second Inaugural Address
March 4, 1865

Fellow-Countrymen:

At this second appearing to take the oath of the Presidential office there is less occasion for an extended address than there was at the first. Then a statement somewhat in detail of a course to be pursued seemed fitting and proper. Now, at the expiration of four years, during which public declarations have been constantly called forth on every point and phase of this great conflict which is of primary concern to the nation as a whole, little that is new could be presented. The progress of our arms, on which all else chiefly depends, is as well known to the public as to myself, and it is, I trust, reasonably satisfactory and encouraging to all. With high hope for the future, no prediction in regard to it is ventured.

On the occasion corresponding to this four years ago, all thoughts were anxiously directed to an impending civil war. All dreaded it, all sought to avert it. While the inaugural address was being delivered from this place, devoted altogether to *saving* the Union without war, insurgent agents were in the city seeking to *destroy* it without war--seeking to dissolve the Union and divide effects by negotiation. Both parties deprecated war, but one of them would *make* war rather than let the nation survive, and the other would *accept* war rather than let it perish. And the war came.

One-eighth of the whole population were colored slaves, not distributed generally over the whole Union, but localized in the southern part of it. These slaves constituted a peculiar and powerful interest. All knew that this interest was somehow the cause of the war. To strengthen, perpetuate, and extend this interest was the object for which the insurgents would rend the Union, even by war, while the Government claimed no right to do more than to restrict the territorial enlargement of it. Neither party expected for the war the magnitude or the duration which it has already attained. Neither anticipated that the *cause* of the conflict might cease with or even before the conflict itself should cease. Each looked for an easier triumph, and a result less fundamental and astounding. Both read the same Bible and pray to the same God, and each invokes His aid against the other. It may seem strange that any men should dare to ask a just God's assistance in wringing their bread from the sweat of other men's faces, but let us judge not that we be not judged. The prayers of both could not be answered. That of neither has been answered fully. The Almighty has His own purposes. "Woe unto the world because of offenses; because it must needs be that offenses come, but woe to the man by whom the offense cometh." If we shall suppose that American slavery is one of those offenses which, in the providence of God, must needs come, but which, having continued through His appointed time, He now wills to remove, and that He gives to both North and South this terrible war as the woe due to those by whom the offense came, shall we discern therein any departure from those divine attributes which the believers in a living God always ascribe to Him? Fondly do we hope, fervently do we pray, that this mighty scourge of war may speedily pass away. Yet if God wills that it continues until all the wealth piled by the bondsman's two hundred and fifty years of unrequited toil shall be sunk, and until every drop of blood drawn with the lash shall be paid with another drawn by the sword, as was said three thousand years ago, so still it must be said "the judgments of the Lord are true and righteous altogether."

With malice toward none, with charity for all, with firmness in the right as God gives us to see the right, let us strive on to finish the work we are in, to bind up the nation's wounds, to care for him who shall have borne the battle and for his widow and his orphan, to do all which may achieve and cherish a just and lasting peace among ourselves and with all nations.

President Franklin Delano Roosevelt
The First Inaugural Address
March 4, 1933

I am certain that my fellow Americans expect that on my induction into the Presidency I will address them with a candor and a decision which the present situation of our Nation impels. This is preeminently the time to speak the truth, the whole truth, frankly and boldly. Nor need we shrink from honestly facing conditions in our country today. This great Nation will endure as it has endured, will revive and will prosper. So first of all, let me assert my firm belief that the only thing we have to fear is fear itself--nameless, unreasoning, unjustified terror which paralyzes needed efforts to convert retreat into advance. In every dark hour of our national life a leadership of frankness and vigor has met with that understanding and support of the people themselves which is essential to victory. I am convinced that you will again give that support to leadership in these critical days.

In such a spirit on my part and on yours we face our common difficulties. They concern, thank God, only material things. Values have shrunken to fantastic levels; taxes have risen; our ability to pay has fallen; government of all kinds is faced by serious curtailment of income; the means of exchange are frozen in the currents of trade; the withered leaves of industrial enterprise lie on every side; farmers find no markets for their produce; the savings of many years in thousands of families are gone.

More important, a host of unemployed citizens face the grim problem of existence, and an equally great number toil with little return. Only a foolish optimist can deny the dark realities of the moment.

Yet our distress comes from no failure of substance. We are stricken by no plague of locusts. Compared with the perils which our forefathers conquered because they believed and were not afraid, we have still much to be thankful for. Nature still offers her bounty and human efforts have multiplied it. Plenty is at our doorstep, but a generous use of it languishes in the very sight of the supply. Primarily this is because the rulers of the exchange of mankind's goods have failed, through their own stubbornness and their own incompetence, have admitted their failure, and abdicated. Practices of the unscrupulous money changers stand indicted in the court of public opinion, rejected by the hearts and minds of men.

True they have tried, but their efforts have been cast in the pattern of an outworn tradition. Faced by failure of credit they have proposed only the lending of more money. Stripped of the lure of profit by which to induce our people to follow their false leadership, they have resorted to exhortations, pleading tearfully for restored confidence. They know only the rules of a generation of self-seekers. They have no vision, and when there is no vision the people perish.

The money changers have fled from their high seats in the temple of our civilization. We may now restore that temple to the ancient truths. The measure of the restoration lies in the extent to which we apply social values more noble than mere monetary profit.

Happiness lies not in the mere possession of money; it lies in the joy of achievement, in the thrill of creative effort. The joy and moral stimulation of work no longer must be forgotten in the mad chase of evanescent profits. These dark days will be worth all they cost us if they teach us that our true destiny is not to be ministered unto but to minister to ourselves and to our fellow men.

Recognition of the falsity of material wealth as the standard of success goes hand in hand with the abandonment of the false belief that public office and high political position are to be valued only by the standards of pride of place and personal profit; and there must be an end to a conduct in banking and in business which too often has given to a sacred trust the likeness of callous and selfish wrongdoing. Small wonder that confidence languishes, for it thrives only on honesty, on honor, on the sacredness of obligations, on faithful protection, on unselfish performance; without them it cannot live.

Restoration calls, however, not for changes in ethics alone. The Nation asks for action, and action now.

Our greatest primary task is to put people to work. This is no unsolvable problem if we face it wisely and courageously. It can be accomplished in part by direct recruiting by the Government itself, treating the task as we would treat the emergency of a war, but at the same time, through this employment, accomplishing greatly needed projects to stimulate and reorganize the use of our natural resources.

Hand in hand with this we must frankly recognize the overbalance of population in our industrial centers and, by engaging on a national scale in a redistribution, endeavor to provide a better use of the land for those best fitted for the land. The task can be helped by definite efforts to raise the values of agricultural products and with this the power to purchase the output of our cities. It can be helped by preventing realistically the tragedy of the growing loss through foreclosure of our small homes and our farms. It can be helped by the insistence that the Federal, State and local governments act forthwith on the demand that their cost be drastically reduced. It can be helped by the unifying of relief activities which today are often scattered, uneconomical, and unequal. It can be helped by national planning for and supervision of all forms of transportation and of communications and other utilities which have a definitely public character. There are many ways in which it can be helped, but it can never be helped merely by talking about it. We must act and act quickly.

Finally, in our progress toward a resumption of work we require two safeguards against a return of the evils of the old order; there must be a strict supervision of all banking and credits and investments; there must be an end to speculation with other people's money, and there must be provision for an adequate but sound currency.

There are the lines of attack. I shall presently urge upon a new Congress in special session detailed measures for their fulfillment, and I shall seek the immediate assistance of the several States.

Through this program of action we address ourselves to putting our own national house in order and making income balance outgo. Our international trade relations, though vastly important, are in point of time and necessity secondary to the establishment of a sound national economy. I favor as a practical policy the practice of putting first things first. I shall spare no effort to restore world trade by international economic readjustment, but the emergency at home cannot wait on that accomplishment.

The basic thought that guides these specific means of national recovery is not narrowly nationalistic. It is the insistence, as a first consideration, upon the interdependence of the various elements in all parts of the United States--a recognition of the old and permanently important manifestation of the American spirit of the pioneer. It is the way to recovery. It is the immediate way. It is the strongest assurance that the recovery will endure.

In the field of world policy I would dedicate this Nation to the policy of the good neighbor--the neighbor who resolutely respects himself and, because he does so, respects the rights of others--the neighbor who respects his obligations and respects the sanctity of his agreements in and with a world of neighbors.

If I read the temper of our people correctly, we now realize as we have never realized before our interdependence on each other; that we cannot merely take but we must give as well; that if we are to go forward, we must move as a trained and loyal army willing to sacrifice for the good of a common discipline, because without such discipline no progress is made, no leadership becomes effective. We are, I know, ready and willing to submit our lives and property to such discipline, because it makes possible a leadership which aims at a larger good. This I propose to offer, pledging that the larger purposes will bind upon us all as a sacred obligation with a unity of duty hitherto evoked only in time of armed strife.

With this pledge taken, I assume unhesitatingly the leadership of this great army of our people dedicated to a disciplined attack upon our common problems.

Action in this image and to this end is feasible under the form of government which we have inherited from our ancestors. Our Constitution is so simple and practical that it is possible always to meet extraordinary needs by changes in emphasis and arrangement without loss of essential form. That is why our constitutional system has proved itself the most superbly enduring political mechanism the modern world has produced. It has met every stress of vast expansion of territory, of foreign wars, of bitter internal strife, of world relations.

It is to be hoped that the normal balance of executive and legislative authority may be wholly adequate to meet the unprecedented task before us. But it may be that an unprecedented demand and need for undelayed action may call for temporary departure from that normal balance of public procedure.

I am prepared under my constitutional duty to recommend the measures that a stricken nation in the midst of a stricken world may require. These measures, or such other measures as the Congress may build out of its experience and wisdom, I shall seek, within my constitutional authority, to bring to speedy adoption.

But in the event that Congress shall fail to take one of these two courses, and in the event that the national emergency is still critical, I shall not evade the clear course of duty that will then confront me. I shall ask the Congress for the one remaining instrument to meet the crisis--broad Executive power to wage a war against the emergency, as great as the power that would be given to me if we were in fact invaded by a foreign foe.

For the trust reposed in me I will return the courage and the devotion that befit the time. I can do no less.

We face the arduous days that lie before us in the warm courage of the national unity; with the clear consciousness of seeking old and precious moral values; with the clean satisfaction that comes from the stern performance of duty by old and young alike. We aim at the assurance of a rounded and permanent national life.

We do not distrust the future of essential democracy. The people of the United States have not failed. In their need they have registered a mandate that they want direct, vigorous action. They have asked for discipline and direction under leadership. They have made me the present instrument of their wishes. In the spirit of the gift I take it.

In this dedication of a Nation we humbly ask the blessing of God. May He protect each and every one of us. May He guide me in the days to come.

President Theodore Roosevelt
Inaugural Address
March 4, 1905

My fellow citizens, no people on earth have more cause to be thankful than ours, and this is said reverently, in no spirit of boastfulness in our own strength, but with gratitude to the Giver of Good who has blessed us with the conditions which have enabled us to achieve so large a measure of well-being and of happiness. To us as a people it has been granted to lay the foundations of our national life in a new continent. We are the heirs of the ages, and yet we have had to pay few of the penalties which in old countries are exacted by the dead hand of a bygone civilization. We have not been obliged to fight for our existence against any alien race; and yet our life has called for the vigor and effort without which the manlier and hardier virtues wither away. Under such conditions it would be our own fault if we failed; and the success we have had in the past, the success which we confidently believe the future will bring, should cause in us no feeling of vainglory, but rather a deep and abiding realization of all which life has offered us; a full acknowledgment of the responsibility which is ours; and a fixed determination to show that under a free government a mighty people can thrive best, alike as regards the things of the body and the things of the soul.

Much has been given us, and much will rightfully be expected from us. We have duties to others and duties to ourselves; and we can shirk neither. We have become a great nation, forced by the fact of its greatness into relations with the other nations of the earth, and we must behave as beseems a people with such responsibilities. Towards all other nations, large and small, our attitude must be one of cordial and sincere friendship. We must show not only in our words, but in our deeds, that we are earnestly desirous of securing their good will by acting toward them in a spirit of just and generous recognition of all their rights. But justice and generosity in a nation, as in an individual, count most when shown not by the weak but by the strong. While ever careful to refrain from wrongdoing others, we must be no less insistent that we are not wronged ourselves. We wish peace, but we wish the peace of justice, the peace of righteousness. We wish it because we think it is right and not because we are afraid. No weak nation that acts manfully and justly should ever have cause to fear us, and no strong power should ever be able to single us out as a subject for insolent aggression.

Our relations with the other powers of the world are important; but still more important are our relations among ourselves. Such growth in wealth, in population, and in power as this nation has seen during the century and a quarter of its national life is inevitably accompanied by a like growth in the problems which are ever before every nation that rises to greatness. Power invariably means both responsibility and danger. Our forefathers faced certain perils which we have outgrown. We now face other perils, the very existence of which it was impossible that they should foresee. Modern life is both complex and intense, and the tremendous changes wrought by the extraordinary industrial development of the last half century are felt in every fiber of our social and political being. Never before have men tried so vast and formidable an experiment as that of administering the affairs of a continent under the forms of a Democratic republic. The conditions which have told for our marvelous material well-being, which have developed to a very high degree our energy, self-reliance, and individual initiative, have also brought the care and anxiety inseparable from the accumulation of great wealth in industrial centers. Upon the success of our experiment much depends, not only as regards our own welfare, but as regards the welfare of mankind. If we fail, the cause of free self-government throughout the world will rock to its foundations, and therefore our responsibility is heavy, to ourselves, to the world as it is to-day, and to the generations yet unborn. There is no good reason why we should fear the future, but there is every reason why we should face it seriously, neither hiding from ourselves the gravity of the problems before us nor fearing to approach these problems with the unbending, unflinching purpose to solve them aright.

Yet, after all, though the problems are new, though the tasks set before us differ from the tasks set before our fathers who founded and preserved this Republic, the spirit in which these tasks must be undertaken and these problems faced, if our duty is to be well done, remains essentially unchanged. We know that self-government is difficult. We know that no people needs such high traits of character as that people which seeks to govern its affairs aright through the freely expressed will of the freemen who compose it. But we have faith that we shall not prove false to the memories of the men of the mighty past. They did their work, they left us the splendid heritage we now enjoy. We in our turn have an assured confidence that we shall be able to leave this heritage unwasted and enlarged to our children and our children's children. To do so we must show, not merely in great crises, but in the everyday affairs of life, the qualities of practical intelligence, of courage, of hardihood, and endurance, and above all the power of devotion to a lofty ideal, which made great the men who founded this Republic in the days of Washington, which made great the men who preserved this Republic in the days of Abraham Lincoln.

President George Washington
Farewell Address
September 19, 1796

Friends and Citizens:

The period for a new election of a citizen to administer the executive government of the United States being not far distant, and the time actually arrived when your thoughts must be employed in designating the person who is to be clothed with that important trust, it appears to me proper, especially as it may conduce to a more distinct expression of the public voice, that I should now apprise you of the resolution I have formed, to decline being considered among the number of those out of whom a choice is to be made.

I beg you, at the same time, to do me the justice to be assured that this resolution has not been taken without a strict regard to all the considerations appertaining to the relation which binds a dutiful citizen to his country; and that in withdrawing the tender of service, which silence in my situation might imply, I am influenced by no diminution of zeal for your future interest, no deficiency of grateful respect for your past kindness, but am supported by a full conviction that the step is compatible with both.

The acceptance of, and continuation hitherto in, the office to which your suffrages have twice called me have been a uniform sacrifice of inclination to the opinion of duty and to a deference for what appeared to be your desire. I constantly hoped that it would have been much earlier in my power, consistently with motives which I was not at liberty to disregard, to return to that retirement from which I had been reluctantly drawn. The strength of my inclination to do this, previous to the last election, had even led to the preparation of an address to declare it to you; but mature reflection on the then perplexed and critical posture of our affairs with foreign nations, and the unanimous advice of persons entitled to my confidence, impelled me to abandon the idea.

I rejoice that the state of your concerns, external as well as internal, no longer renders the pursuit of inclination incompatible with the sentiment of duty or propriety, and am persuaded, whatever partiality may be retained for my services, that, in the present circumstances of our country, you will not disapprove my determination to retire.

The impressions with which I first undertook the arduous trust were explained on the proper occasion. In the discharge of this trust, I will only say that I have, with good intentions, contributed towards the organization and administration of the government the best exertions of which a very fallible judgment was capable. Not unconscious in the outset of the inferiority of my qualifications, experience in my own eyes, perhaps still more in the eyes of others, has strengthened the motives to diffidence of myself; and every day the increasing weight of years admonishes me more and more that the shade of retirement is as necessary to me as it will be welcome. Satisfied that if any circumstances have given peculiar value to my services, they were temporary, I have the consolation to believe that, while choice and prudence invite me to quit the political scene, patriotism does not forbid it.

In looking forward to the moment which is intended to terminate the career of my public life, my feelings do not permit me to suspend the deep acknowledgment of that debt of gratitude which I owe to my beloved country for the many honors it has conferred upon me; still more for the steadfast confidence with which it has supported me; and for the opportunities I have thence enjoyed of manifesting my inviolable attachment, by services faithful and persevering, though in usefulness unequal to my zeal. If benefits have resulted to our country from these services, let it always be remembered to your praise, and as an instructive example in our annals, that under circumstances in which the passions, agitated in every direction, were liable to mislead, amidst appearances sometimes dubious, vicissitudes of fortune often discouraging, in situations in which not unfrequently want of success has countenanced the spirit of criticism, the constancy of your support was the essential prop of the efforts, and a guarantee of the plans by which they were effected. Profoundly penetrated with this idea, I shall carry it with me to my grave, as a strong incitement to unceasing vows that heaven may continue to you the choicest tokens of its beneficence; that your union and brotherly affection may be perpetual; that the free Constitution, which is the work of your hands, may be sacredly maintained; that its administration in every department may be stamped with wisdom and virtue; that, in fine, the happiness of the people of these States, under the auspices of liberty, may be made complete by so careful a preservation and so prudent a use of this blessing as will acquire to them the glory of recommending it to the applause, the affection, and adoption of every nation which is yet a stranger to it.

Here, perhaps, I ought to stop. But a solicitude for your welfare, which cannot end but with my life, and the apprehension of danger, natural to that solicitude, urge me, on an occasion like the present, to offer to your solemn contemplation, and to recommend to your frequent review, some sentiments which are the result of much reflection, of no inconsiderable observation, and which appear to me all-important to the permanency of your felicity as a people. These will be offered to you with the more freedom, as you can only see in them the disinterested warnings of a parting friend, who can possibly have no personal motive to bias his counsel. Nor can I forget, as an encouragement to it, your indulgent reception of my sentiments on a former and not dissimilar occasion.

Interwoven as is the love of liberty with every ligament of your hearts, no recommendation of mine is necessary to fortify or confirm the attachment.

The unity of government which constitutes you one people is also now dear to you. It is justly so, for it is a main pillar in the edifice of your real independence, the support of your tranquility at home, your peace abroad; of your safety; of your prosperity; of that very liberty which you so highly prize. But as it is easy to foresee that, from different causes and from different quarters, much pains will be taken, many artifices employed to weaken in your minds the conviction of this truth; as this is the point in your political fortress against which the batteries of internal and external enemies will be most constantly and actively (though often covertly and insidiously) directed, it is of infinite moment that you should properly estimate the immense value of your national union to your collective and individual happiness; that you should cherish a cordial, habitual, and immovable attachment to it; accustoming yourselves to think and speak of it as of the palladium of your political safety and prosperity; watching for its preservation with jealous anxiety; discountenancing whatever may suggest even a suspicion that it can in any event be abandoned; and indignantly frowning upon the first dawning of every attempt to alienate any portion of our country from the rest, or to enfeeble the sacred ties which now link together the various parts.

For this you have every inducement of sympathy and interest. Citizens, by birth or choice, of a common country, that country has a right to concentrate your affections. The name of American, which belongs to you in your national capacity, must always exalt the just pride of patriotism more than any appellation derived from local discriminations. With slight shades of difference, you have the same religion, manners, habits, and political principles. You have in a common cause fought and triumphed together; the independence and liberty you possess are the work of joint counsels, and joint efforts of common dangers, sufferings, and successes.

But these considerations, however powerfully they address themselves to your sensibility, are greatly outweighed by those which apply more immediately to your interest. Here every portion of our country finds the most commanding motives for carefully guarding and preserving the union of the whole.

The North, in an unrestrained intercourse with the South, protected by the equal laws of a common government, finds in the productions of the latter great additional resources of maritime and commercial enterprise and precious materials of manufacturing industry. The South, in the same intercourse, benefiting by the agency of the North, sees its agriculture grow and its commerce expand. Turning partly into its own channels the seamen of the North, it finds its particular navigation invigorated; and, while it contributes, in different ways, to nourish an increase the general mass of the national navigation, it looks forward to the protection of a maritime strength, to which itself is unequally adapted. The East, in a like intercourse with the West, already finds, and in the progressive improvement of interior communications by land and water, will more and more find a valuable vent for the commodities which it brings from abroad, or manufactures at home. The West derives from the East supplies requisite to its growth and comfort, and, what is perhaps of still greater consequence, it must of necessity owe the secure enjoyment of indispensable outlets for its own productions to the weight, influence, and the future maritime strength of the Atlantic side of the Union, directed by an indissoluble community of interest as one nation. Any other tenure by which the West can hold this essential advantage, whether derived from its own separate strength, or from an apostate and unnatural connection with any foreign power, must be intrinsically precarious.

While, then, every part of our country thus feels an immediate and particular interest in union, all the parts combined cannot fail to find in the united mass of means and efforts greater strength, greater resource, proportionably greater security from external danger, a less frequent interruption of their peace by foreign nations; and, what is of inestimable value, they must derive from union an exemption from those broils and wars between themselves, which so frequently afflict neighboring countries not tied together by the same governments, which their own rival ships alone would be sufficient to produce, but which opposite foreign alliances, attachments, and intrigues would stimulate and embitter. Hence, likewise, they will avoid the necessity of those overgrown military establishments which, under any form of government, are inauspicious to liberty, and which are to be regarded as particularly hostile to republican liberty. In this sense it is that your union ought to be considered as a main prop of your liberty, and that the love of the one ought to endear to you the preservation of the other.

These considerations speak a persuasive language to every reflecting and virtuous mind, and exhibit the continuation of the Union as a primary object of patriotic desire. Is there a doubt whether a common government can embrace so large a sphere? Let experience solve it. To listen to mere speculation in such a case were criminal. We are authorized to hope that a proper organization of the whole with the auxiliary agency of governments for the respective subdivisions, will afford a happy issue to the experiment. It is well worth a fair and full experiment. With such powerful and obvious motives to union, affecting all parts of our country, while experience shall not have demonstrated its impracticability, there will always be reason to distrust the patriotism of those who in any quarter may endeavor to weaken its bands.

In contemplating the causes which may disturb our Union, it occurs as matter of serious concern that any ground should have been furnished for characterizing parties by geographical discriminations, Northern and Southern, Atlantic and Western; whence designing men may endeavor to excite a belief that there is a real difference of local interests and views. One of the expedients of party to acquire influence within particular districts is to misrepresent the opinions and aims of other districts. You cannot shield yourself too much against the jealousies and heartburnings which spring from these misrepresentations; they tend to render alien to each other those who ought to be bound together by fraternal affection. The inhabitants of our Western country have lately had a useful lesson on this head; they have seen, in the negotiation by the Executive, and in the unanimous ratification by the Senate, of the treaty with Spain, and in the universal satisfaction at that event, throughout the United States, a decisive proof how unfounded were the suspicions propagated among them of a policy in the General Government and in the Atlantic States unfriendly to their interests in regard to the Mississippi; they have been witnesses to the formation of two treaties, that with Great Britain, and that with Spain, which secure to them everything they could desire, in respect to our foreign relations, towards confirming their prosperity. Will it not be their wisdom to rely for the preservation of these advantages on the Union by which they were procured? Will they not henceforth be deaf to those advisers, if such there are, who would sever them from their brethren and connect them with aliens?

To the efficacy and permanency of your Union, a government for the whole is indispensable. No alliance, however strict, between the parts can be an adequate substitute; they must inevitably experience the infractions and interruptions which all alliances in all times have experienced. Sensible of this momentous truth, you have improved upon you first essay, by the adoption of a constitution of government better calculated than your former for an intimate union, and for the efficacious management of your common concerns. This government, the offspring of our own choice, uninfluenced and unawed, adopted upon full investigation and mature deliberation, completely free in its principles, in the distribution of its powers, uniting security with energy, and containing within itself a provision for its own amendment, has a just claim to your confidence and your support. Respect for its authority, compliance with its laws, acquiescence in its measures, are duties enjoined by the fundamental maxims of true liberty. The basis of our political systems is the right of the people to make and to alter their constitutions of government. But the Constitution which at any time exists, till changed by an explicit and authentic act of the whole people, is sacredly obligatory upon all. The very idea of the power and the right of the people to establish government presupposes the duty of every individual to obey the established government.

All obstructions to the execution of the laws, all combinations and associations, under whatever plausible character, with the real design to direct, control, counteract, or awe the regular deliberation and action of the constituted authorities, are destructive of this fundamental principle, and of fatal tendency. They serve to organize faction, to give it an artificial and extraordinary force; to put, in the place of the delegated will of the nation the will of a party, often a small but artful and enterprising minority of the community; and, according to the alternate triumphs of different parties, to make the public administration the mirror of the ill-concerted and incongruous projects of faction, rather than the organ of consistent and wholesome plans digested by common counsels and modified by mutual interests.

However combinations or associations of the above description may now and then answer popular ends, they are likely, in the course of time and things, to become potent engines, by which cunning, ambitious, and unprincipled men will be enabled to subvert the power of the people and to usurp for themselves the reins of government, destroying afterwards the very engines which have lifted them to unjust dominion.

Towards the preservation of your government, and the permanency of your present happy state, it is requisite, not only that you steadily discountenance irregular oppositions to its acknowledged authority, but also that you resist with care the spirit of innovation upon its principles, however specious the pretexts. One method of assault may be to effect, in the forms of the Constitution, alterations which will impair the energy of the system, and thus to undermine what cannot be directly overthrown. In all the changes to which you may be invited, remember that time and habit are at least as necessary to fix the true character of governments as of other human institutions; that experience is the surest standard by which to test the real tendency of the existing constitution of a country; that facility in changes, upon the credit of mere hypothesis and opinion, exposes to perpetual change, from the endless variety of hypothesis and opinion; and remember, especially, that for the efficient management of your common interests, in a country so extensive as ours, a government of as much vigor as is consistent with the perfect security of liberty is indispensable. Liberty itself will find in such a government, with powers properly distributed and adjusted, its surest guardian. It is, indeed, little else than a name, where the government is too feeble to withstand the enterprises of faction, to confine each member of the society within the limits prescribed by the laws, and to maintain all in the secure and tranquil enjoyment of the rights of person and property.

I have already intimated to you the danger of parties in the State, with particular reference to the founding of them on geographical discriminations. Let me now take a more comprehensive view, and warn you in the most solemn manner against the baneful effects of the spirit of party generally.

This spirit, unfortunately, is inseparable from our nature, having its root in the strongest passions of the human mind. It exists under different shapes in all governments, more or less stifled, controlled, or repressed; but, in those of the popular form, it is seen in its greatest rankness, and is truly their worst enemy.

The alternate domination of one faction over another, sharpened by the spirit of revenge, natural to party dissension, which in different ages and countries has perpetrated the most horrid enormities, is itself a frightful despotism. But this leads at length to a more formal and permanent despotism. The disorders and miseries which result gradually incline the minds of men to seek security and repose in the absolute power of an individual; and sooner or later the chief of some prevailing faction, more able or more fortunate than his competitors, turns this disposition to the purposes of his own elevation, on the ruins of public liberty.

Without looking forward to an extremity of this kind (which nevertheless ought not to be entirely out of sight), the common and continual mischiefs of the spirit of party are sufficient to make it the interest and duty of a wise people to discourage and restrain it.

It serves always to distract the public councils and enfeeble the public administration. It agitates the community with ill-founded jealousies and false alarms, kindles the animosity of one part against another, foments occasionally riot and insurrection. It opens the door to foreign influence and corruption, which finds a facilitated access to the government itself through the channels of party passions. Thus the policy and the will of one country are subjected to the policy and will of another.

There is an opinion that parties in free countries are useful checks upon the administration of the government and serve to keep alive the spirit of liberty. This within certain limits is probably true; and in governments of a monarchical cast, patriotism may look with indulgence, if not with favor, upon the spirit of party. But in those of the popular character, in governments purely elective, it is a spirit not to be encouraged. From their natural tendency, it is certain there will always be enough of that spirit for every salutary purpose. And there being constant danger of excess, the effort ought to be by force of public opinion, to mitigate and assuage it. A fire not to be quenched, it demands a uniform vigilance to prevent its bursting into a flame, lest, instead of warming, it should consume.

It is important, likewise, that the habits of thinking in a free country should inspire caution in those entrusted with its administration, to confine themselves within their respective constitutional spheres, avoiding in the exercise of the powers of one department to encroach upon another. The spirit of encroachment tends to consolidate the powers of all the departments in one, and thus to create, whatever the form of government, a real despotism. A just estimate of that love of power, and proneness to abuse it, which predominates in the human heart, is sufficient to satisfy us of the truth of this position. the necessity of reciprocal checks in the exercise of political power, by dividing and distributing it into different depositaries, and constituting each the guardian of the public weal against invasions by the others, has been evinced by experiments ancient and modern; some of them in our country and under our own eyes. To preserve them must be as necessary as to institute them. If, in the opinion of the people, the distribution or modification of the constitutional powers be in any particular wrong, let it be corrected by an amendment in the way which the Constitution designates. But let there be no change by usurpation; for though this, in one instance, may be the instrument of good, it is the customary weapon by which free governments are destroyed. The precedent must always greatly overbalance in permanent evil any partial or transient benefit, which the use can at any time yield.

Of all the dispositions and habits which lead to political prosperity, religion and morality are indispensable supports. In vain would that man claim the tribute of patriotism, who should labor to subvert these great pillars of human happiness, these firmest props of the duties of men and citizens. The mere politician, equally with the pious man, ought to respect and to cherish them. A volume could not trace all their connections with private and public felicity. Let it simply be asked: Where is the security for property, for reputation, for life, if the sense of religious obligation desert the oaths which are the instruments of investigation in courts of justice? And let us with caution indulge the supposition that morality can be maintained without religion. Whatever may be conceded to the influence of refined education on minds of peculiar structure, reason and experience both forbid us to expect that national morality can prevail in exclusion of religious principle.

It is substantially true that virtue or morality is a necessary spring of popular government. The rule, indeed, extends with more or less force to every species of free government. Who that is a sincere friend to it can look with indifference upon attempts to shake the foundation of the fabric?

Promote then, as an object of primary importance, institutions for the general diffusion of knowledge. In proportion as the structure of a government gives force to public opinion, it is essential that public opinion should be enlightened.

As a very important source of strength and security, cherish public credit. One method of preserving it is to use it as sparingly as possible, avoiding occasions of expense by cultivating peace, but remembering also that timely disbursements to prepare for danger frequently prevent much greater disbursements to repel it, avoiding likewise the accumulation of debt, not only by shunning occasions of expense, but by vigorous exertion in time of peace to discharge the debts which unavoidable wars may have occasioned, not ungenerously throwing upon posterity the burden which we ourselves ought to bear. The execution of these maxims belongs to your representatives, but it is necessary that public opinion should co-operate. To facilitate to them the performance of their duty, it is essential that you should practically bear in mind that towards the payment of debts there must be revenue; that to have revenue there must be taxes; that no taxes can be devised which are not more or less inconvenient and unpleasant; that the intrinsic embarrassment, inseparable from the selection of the proper objects (which is always a choice of difficulties), ought to be a decisive motive for a candid construction of the conduct of the government in making it, and for a spirit of acquiescence in the measures for obtaining revenue, which the public exigencies may at any time dictate.

Observe good faith and justice towards all nations; cultivate peace and harmony with all. Religion and morality enjoin this conduct; and can it be, that good policy does not equally enjoin it - It will be worthy of a free, enlightened, and at no distant period, a great nation, to give mankind the magnanimous and too novel example of a people always guided by an exalted justice and benevolence. Who can doubt that, in the course of time and things, the fruits of such a plan would richly repay any temporary advantages which might be lost by a steady adherence to it? Can it be that Providence has not connected the permanent felicity of a nation with its virtue? The experiment, at least, is recommended by every sentiment which ennobles human nature. Alas! is it rendered impossible by its vices?

In the execution of such a plan, nothing is more essential than that permanent, inveterate antipathies against particular nations, and passionate attachments for others, should be excluded; and that, in place of them, just and amicable feelings towards all should be cultivated. The nation which indulges towards another a habitual hatred or a habitual fondness is in some degree a slave. It is a slave to its animosity or to its affection, either of which is sufficient to lead it astray from its duty and its interest. Antipathy in one nation against another disposes each more readily to offer insult and injury, to lay hold of slight causes of umbrage, and to be haughty and intractable, when accidental or trifling occasions of dispute occur. Hence, frequent collisions, obstinate, envenomed, and bloody contests. The nation, prompted by ill-will and resentment, sometimes impels to war the government, contrary to the best calculations of policy. The government sometimes participates in the national propensity, and adopts through passion what reason would reject; at other times it makes the animosity of the nation subservient to projects of hostility instigated by pride, ambition, and other sinister and pernicious motives. The peace often, sometimes perhaps the liberty, of nations, has been the victim.

So likewise, a passionate attachment of one nation for another produces a variety of evils. Sympathy for the favorite nation, facilitating the illusion of an imaginary common interest in cases where no real common interest exists, and infusing into one the enmities of the other, betrays the former into a participation in the quarrels and wars of the latter without adequate inducement or justification. It leads also to concessions to the favorite nation of privileges denied to others which is apt doubly to injure the nation making the concessions; by unnecessarily parting with what ought to have been retained, and by exciting jealousy, ill-will, and a disposition to retaliate, in the parties from whom equal privileges are withheld. And it gives to ambitious, corrupted, or deluded citizens (who devote themselves to the favorite nation), facility to betray or sacrifice the interests of their own country, without odium, sometimes even with popularity; gilding, with the appearances of a virtuous sense of obligation, a commendable deference for public opinion, or a laudable zeal for public good, the base or foolish compliances of ambition, corruption, or infatuation.

As avenues to foreign influences in innumerable ways, such attachments are particularly alarming to the truly enlightened and independent patriot. How many opportunities do they afford to tamper with domestic factions, to practice the arts of seduction, to mislead public opinion, to influence or awe the public Councils! Such an attachment of a small or weak towards a great & powerful Nation dooms the former to be the satellite of the latter.

Against the insidious wiles of foreign influence (I conjure you to believe me, fellow citizens) the jealousy of a free people ought to be constantly awake, since history and experience prove that foreign influence is one of the most baneful foes of republican government. But that jealousy to be useful must be impartial; else it becomes the instrument of the very influence to be avoided, instead of a defense against it. Excessive partiality for one foreign nation and excessive dislike of another cause those whom they activate to see danger only on one side, and serve to veil and even second the arts of influence on the other. Real Patriots who may resist the intrigues of the favorite are liable to become suspected and odious, while its tools and dupes usurp the applause & confidence of the people, to surrender their interests.

The great rule of conduct for us in regards to foreign nations is in extending our commercial relations, to have with them as little *political* connection as possible. So far as we have already formed engagements, let them be fulfilled with perfect good faith. Here let us stop. Europe has a set of primary interests which to us have none; or a very remote relation. Hence she must be engaged in frequent controversies, the causes of which are essentially foreign to our concerns. Hence, therefore, it must be unwise in us to implicate ourselves by artificial ties in the ordinary vicissitudes of her politics, or the ordinary combinations & collisions of her friendships or enmities.

Our detached & distant situation invites and enables us to pursue a different course. If we remain one People, under an efficient government, the period is not far off, when we may defy material injury from external annoyance; when we may take such an attitude as will cause the neutrality we may at any time resolve upon to be scrupulously respected; when belligerent nations, under the impossibility of making acquisitions upon us, will not lightly hazard the giving us provocation; when we may choose peace or War, as our interest guided by justice shall counsel.

Why forego the advantages of so peculiar a situation? Why quit our own to stand upon foreign ground? Why, by interweaving our destiny with that of any part of Europe, entangle our peace and prosperity in the toils of European ambition, Rivalship, Interest, Humour, or Caprice?

'Tis our true policy to steer clear of permanent Alliances, with any portion of the foreign world--So far, I mean, as we are now at liberty to do it--for let me not be understood as capable of patronising infidility to existing engagements. (I hold the maxim no less applicable to public than to private affairs, that honesty is always the best policy). I repeat it therefore, let those engagements be observed in their genuine sense. But in my opinion, it is unnecessary and would be unwise to extend them.

Taking care always to keep ourselves, by suitable establishments, on a respectably defensive posture, we may safely trust to temporary alliances for extraordinary emergencies.

Harmony, liberal intercourse with all Nations, are recommended by policy, humanity and interest. But even our Commercial policy should hold an equal and impartial hand: neither seeking nor granting exclusive favours or preferences; consulting the natural course of things; diffusing & diversifying by gentle means the streams of Commerce, but forcing nothing; establishing, with Powers so disposed--in order to give trade a stable course, to define the rights of our merchants, and to enable the Government to support them--conventional rules of intercourse, the best that present circumstances and mutual opinion will permit, but temporary, & liable to be from time to time abandoned and varied, as experience and circumstances shall dictate; constantly keeping in view; that 'tis folly in one Nation to look for disinterested favors from another--that it must pay with a portion of its Independence for whatever it may accept under that character--that by such acceptance, it may place itself in the condition of having given equivalents for nominal favours and yet of being reproached with ingratitude for not giving more.

CHAPTER 6

Welcome to the Seventh Party System

The Constitution makes no provision for political parties, but they developed naturally based on different visions for how the government of United States should work. There have been several realignments of political parties since the ratification of the United States Constitution. Political scientists generally describe six distinct party systems from the beginning of the United States to the present day. There is some disagreement over whether, or when, a Seventh Party System may have gone into effect. The first three party systems, which evolved between 1789 and 1896, primarily reflect different views on the powers of the federal government regarding a national bank, use of federal funds for internal improvements, and slavery. From the Fourth Party System through the Sixth Party System, distinctions between the two major parties focused mainly on the degree to which the federal government should control business, protections for those at the lower end of the economic spectrum, and the role the United States should play in the international arena. After describing the evolution of the first six party systems, I will defend the proposition that the Seventh Party System began in the 1990s. The characteristics of this Seventh Party System include a deregulated information stream that has overwhelmed American voters with misinformation, and the acceptance of white supremacist, neo-Nazi and authoritarian ideologies within the Republican Party.

The First Party System (1792-1824) consisted of the Federalist Party and the Democratic-Republican Party. These parties reflected the two sides of the debate (from the Constitutional Convention) over how much power to give the executive branch in the new United States government. The Federalist Party was dominant until about 1800, after which the Democratic-Republicans gained the upper hand.

The issue that is often used to differentiate Federalists from Democratic-Republicans is that of the national bank. As the first Secretary of the Treasury, Alexander Hamilton favored the national bank, the assumption of state debts by the federal government, and a tariff to provide funds for paying the consolidated debt. These were hallmarks of the Federalist Party, along with support for business interests and manufacturing. Federalists favored stronger relations with Great Britain over relations with France based on trade relations and political stability. After 1816, the Federalist Party was not a significant participant in national elections, and the Democratic-Republican Party was left as the only major party for a short period.

The Democratic-Republican Party was led initially by Thomas Jefferson and James Madison. This party opposed strong executive power, the national bank and a strong standing military. Democratic-Republicans were aligned with agricultural interests. They supported the French Revolution and preferred closer ties to France. Although they were commonly referred to as Republicans, they have no connection to the Republican party that emerged in the Civil War era.

The Second Party System (mid 1820s - mid1850s) evolved as the Democratic-Republicans split into the Democratic Party and the National Republican Party. Andrew Jackson was the leader of the Democratic Party, while John Quincy Adams and Henry Clay led the National Republicans. The Second Party System also had some minor parties: the Anti-Masonic Party, the abolitionist Liberty Party and the anti-slavery Free Soil Party.

In 1833, the National Republican Party merged with the Anti-Masonic Party and became the Whig Party. The Whigs opposed territorial expansion and the war with Mexico. They favored a strong Congress and opposed strong presidents (like Jackson). Whigs favored protective tariffs, federal funding for infrastructure projects, and a national bank. At its beginning, the party existed in both the North and the South, and had no unified position on slavery.

Jackson's Democratic Party was a populist, anti-elite party that was in favor of territorial expansion, agrarianism and expanding the vote to all white males (with no property requirement). The party was a coalition of white men with little economic or political power, including small farmers, urban laborers and Irish Catholics. Jacksonian Democrats did not support a national bank because they believed government involvement in the economy favored the rich. In general, they viewed the federal government as the enemy of individual liberty.

The Third Party System (mid 1850s - mid 1890s) evolved as conflict over slavery splintered both the Whig Party and the Democratic Party. Anti-slavery Whigs like Abraham Lincoln formed the nucleus of the new Republican Party while pro-slavery Whigs migrated to the highly nationalistic and anti-immigrant American Party or the Constitutional Union Party. Both the American Party and the Constitutional Union Party dissolved at the beginning of the Civil War. The split in the Democratic Party was mostly between southerners who insisted on their right to bring slavery into the new western territories and northerners who supported the idea that new territories should become slave or free based on elections held in the territories themselves. The two sides could not agree on a nominee for the presidential election of 1860. Lincoln's victory in that election led to secession by several states. After the Civil War, the Democratic Party struggled to reassert itself at the federal level but remained the party of the "solid South" until well into the twentieth century.

Following the defeat of the confederate southern states in the Civil War, the Republican Party dominated the federal government for most of the Third Party System era. Grover Cleveland, who served non-consecutive terms from 1885-1889 and 1893-1897, was the only Democratic president during this period. Republicans controlled the Senate for all but four years (1878-80 and 1892-94). Control of the House of Representatives was more evenly split. A major economic depression powered the Democrats to win control of the House in 1874. Overall, Democrats controlled the House for eighteen years and Republicans held the majority for fourteen years. A number of smaller parties played a role in the Third Party System era, including the Greenback Party, the Populist Party, the Readjuster Party, and the Silver Republican Party.

The Fourth Party System (1896-1932) involved a change in the issue emphasis of the existing Democratic and Republican parties. As the Civil War veterans grew older, a new cohort of younger voters emerged with a new set of issue priorities in both parties. While the issue of racial injustice persisted, the tremendous expansion of railroads and industrial capitalism created other issues that became more prominent. On the domestic front, these included the role of labor unions, child labor, women's suffrage, prohibition, government regulation of railroads and large corporations, and monetary policy (gold standard versus silver). Within both parties, progressive elements favored reforms in these issue areas.

The Republican Party continued its dominance of the national political scene under the Fourth Party System, controlling both houses of Congress for 28 out of 36 years and at least one house for 30 out of 36 years. Except for Woodrow Wilson, Republican presidents served continuously during this period. In the election of 1912, the progressive wing of the Republican Party split to form the Bull Moose Party with Theodore Roosevelt as its presidential candidate. This split the Republican vote between Roosevelt and Taft, contributing to the election of Woodrow Wilson and to Democrats briefly gaining control of Congress. Republicans regained control of Congress and the White House in the post-war elections of 1918 and 1920. Other minor parties with a role in the Fourth Party System included the Socialist Party, the Prohibition Party, the Popular Party, and the Silver Party.

The onset of the Great Depression in America in 1929, along with the failure of Herbert Hoover's response to it, led to the realignment that created the Fifth Party System (1932-1976). Since the Republicans had control of both houses of Congress after 1918 and complete control of the federal government after 1920, and Hoover had served as Secretary of Commerce from 1921, it was impossible for Republicans to evade responsibility for the near-total collapse of the U.S. economy in 1929. Democrat Franklin Delano Roosevelt won the presidential election of 1932 in a landslide, and Democrats regained control of both houses of Congress.

Although the Democratic Party dominated the federal government for most of the Fifth Party System period, there were Republican presidents from 1952 to 1960 (Dwight Eisenhower) and from 1968 to 1976 (Richard Nixon, Gerald Ford). Democrats also controlled both houses of Congress for most of this period. Republicans controlled both houses of Congress from 1947 to 1949 and from 1953-1955.

As this period progressed, conflict over civil rights, an unpopular war in Vietnam, abortion and a political scandal caused significant shifts in voter allegiance. The Supreme Court decision in *Brown versus Board of Education of Topeka* (1954) ruled segregation in public schools unconstitutional. Democratic president Lyndon Johnson joined with a Democratic majority in Congress to pass the Civil Right Act of 1964. These events caused southern white voters who favored segregation to begin supporting Republican candidates, ending the era of the so-called solid South. Many young people joined mass protests against the war in Vietnam and sought ways to avoid the draft. The Supreme Court decision in *Roe versus Wade* (1973) provided that the Constitution protected a woman's right to have an abortion. In response, an element that came to be known as the "religious right" (many of whom--Catholics and evangelical Christians--had been traditionally Democratic voters) shifted to support Republican candidates. President Richard Nixon's involvement with an attempted break-in at the Democratic National Headquarters (Watergate) during the 1972 election led to his forced resignation on August 8, 1974. Vice President Gerald Ford assumed the Presidency and completed Nixon's term.

The ideological conflicts that brought about the end of the Fifth Party System caused significant political violence. President John F. Kennedy was assassinated in 1963. Public protests over civil rights and against the war in Vietnam often turned violent. Particularly infamous incidents included Alabama police killing and beating peaceful civil rights protesters marching from Selma to Montgomery in 1965, and the Ohio National Guard killing four students in an antiwar protest at Kent State University in 1970. The assassination of civil rights leader Martin Luther King in April of 1968 was followed a few months later by the assassination of Robert Kennedy, the presumptive Democratic nominee for president.

The economy was the major issue at the start of the Fifth Party System; abortion, civil rights, and the Watergate scandal joined the economy as major domestic issues by the end of the period. Foreign policy issues also played a major role as this period progressed: World War II, the Cold War, the nuclear arms race, the Korean War, the Apollo space missions, the Vietnam War, and the Arab Oil Embargo were all major events. Initially, FDR's New Deal coalition comprised a strong majority that included Americans devastated by the Great Depression and the poorly regulated capitalism that led to it. Eventually, a younger generation, having grown up with the New Deal in place, had a lower sense of the significance of hard-won programs like social security, federal deposit insurance, and unemployment insurance. Many Americans lost confidence in a federal government that committed Americans to an un-winnable war in Vietnam, supported dictators in other countries as part of its Cold War strategy, and struggled to meet the economic crisis brought on by the Arab Oil Embargo.

In the 1970s, a series of setbacks in the international arena caused economic trouble at home and a sense that America had lost some of its influence abroad, fostering a segment of voters seeking more forceful presidential leadership. U.S. support for Israel had long been a point of friction with the Arab world. In October of 1973, American aid shipments during the Yom Kippur War sparked an Arab Oil Embargo that rocked the global economy. In April and May of 1975, the fall of regimes supported by the United States and a costly attempt to free the crew of the Mayaguez (a U.S.-flagged merchant ship seized by rebels) underscored the sense that America was unable or unwilling to impose its desired order in Southeast Asia. Elsewhere, in August of 1976, North Korean guards murdered two American officers during a hand-to-hand fight in the Korean Demilitarized Zone (DMZ). Iranian students seized the American embassy in Tehran on November 4, 1979, and held fifty-two Americans hostage for more than a year. The very next month, the Soviet invasion of Afghanistan on Christmas Eve closed a decade of significant setbacks for U.S. interests abroad.

The shift to the Sixth Party System (1976 - 1996) reflected significant changes in voter tendencies arising from the turbulence of the 1960s and 70s. The rise of the religious right to confront the federal government's acknowledgment of a woman's right to abortion brought greater public attention to the effect of presidential elections on the composition of the Supreme Court. The disaffection of southern white voters with the civil rights legislation enacted by the Democratic Party of the 1960s shifted many southern states into the Republican camp. Across the political spectrum, Americans sought federal leadership that they perceived could competently address the economic and foreign policy challenges that plagued the United States in the 1970s. All of this combined to shift white working class and rural voters into a new Republican base, while the Democrats increasingly relied on the vote of minorities, white urban progressives, and college-educated voters.

The Republican Party controlled the White House for twelve of the twenty years between 1976 and 1996; the Democratic Party controlled both houses of Congress for all but the six years between 1981 and 1987 when Republicans gained control of the Senate. In spite of the split control of the executive and legislative branches of the federal government, the World War II generation was still firmly in control of leadership positions in Congress, and there was a greater acceptance of bipartisan initiatives than is common today. In 1976, three years after the *Roe v. Wade* decision, a Democratic-majority Congress passed the Hyde amendment to the Health and Human Services budget. This amendment, sponsored by Republican Congressman Henry Hyde, prohibited the use of federal funds for abortion. The Hyde amendment was reauthorized every year from 1976 until the recent Supreme Court decision overturned *Roe v. Wade*.

During the Sixth Party System era, Republican platforms generally endorsed smaller government, tax cuts, strengthening the military, opposition to abortion, and what came to be known as the "war on drugs". Democratic Party platforms focused on civil rights, universal health care insurance, regulating business to support labor unions and prevent monopolies, and education. Each party criticized the other's efforts. Republicans emphasized individual freedom and criticized the Democrats' for being soft on defense and for creating a culture of dependency through welfare. Democrats countered by contending they were fighting to level the playing field for the working class. Republicans tended to talk about tax cuts and spending cuts, while Democrats tended to talk about attacking fraud and waste in current programs. Republicans talked about family values in the sense of increasing parental control over education and a constitutional amendment to guarantee the right to life of the unborn. Democrats talked about family values through access to health care (including contraception and abortion) and advocacy of child care and other programs to help working women.

During this period, developments in technology, foreign affairs, and communications foreshadowed events that would significantly affect and change American society. Small personal computers hit the market and quickly gained popularity. Instability in the Middle East continued, exacerbating factional fighting that destabilized Lebanon and fostered the spread of Islamic terrorists. The fall of the Berlin Wall in November of 1989 marked the beginning of the end of the Cold War. The U.S. response to the Iraqi invasion of Kuwait in 1990 demonstrated the overwhelming superiority of American military technology. By 1991, with the end of the Soviet Union leaving the U.S. as the sole superpower, the government began efforts to reduce the size of America's Cold War military establishment. In the domestic arena, the deregulation of television and radio began with the Cable Communications Policy Act in 1984, opening the door for a broader selection of channels that could cater to the preferences of more segments of the population. By 1996, the Telecommunications Act enabled the rise of celebrity broadcasters in television and radio who could define and spin news to achieve higher viewership and ratings, thereby attracting more advertising dollars.

In my opinion, the deregulation of television and radio laid the foundation for a new, Seventh Party System beginning in the 1990s. The primary feature of this new party system is a fractured electorate overwhelmed with more information than at any time in human history. Much of the information is contradictory. Many people are unable to discern more reasonable from less reasonable positions for themselves, and fall back on dogmatic frameworks like religion and (often incorrect) perceptions of party identity to simplify their world. Others simply default to the prevailing wisdom of their circle of relatives, friends and coworkers. The ability of almost everyone to find support for conflicting positions on just about any subject fosters distrust of government and political parties.

From the perspective of the major political parties, this new reality increases the importance of their marketing relative to the actual substance of the party message. Messages that are simple, catchy or better funded are likely to win out over more complicated messaging, even when the more complicated message is more reasonable. The net result is an anti-elite, anti-intellectual electorate subject to manipulation by whomever can afford the most marketing.

Perhaps the clearest example of simple messaging winning over more reasonable positions is gun control. Under the Seventh Party System, Republicans tend to support the simple line that any gun control is a violation of the Second Amendment and is therefore unconstitutional.

The epidemic of mass shootings, often by people whose background should have provided reasons to deny them access to the weapons and accessories they used in their crimes, has led to numerous attempts to create reasonable restrictions on the right to own guns. In the Seventh Party System era, it is the Democratic Party that finds itself arguing for things like background checks, restrictions on magazine size and other limits on gun ownership. The National Rifle Association and other pro-gun lobbying groups are a powerful resource for Republican opposition to these initiatives.

The power of marketing is directly tied to the amount of money one can spend to project a message, and the Supreme Court has gutted the campaign finance controls that were in place at the start of the Seventh Party System. In their *Citizens United* and *McCutcheon versus FEC* decisions, the Supreme Court has opened the door for virtually unlimited campaign contributions from various entities that can mask the political agenda of the donors. In recent years, we have found that some of this dark money has found its way into the pockets of the Supreme Court Justices themselves, in ways that should make us all pause. Simple messages powered by lots of dark money and fed through a wide variety of deregulated information channels create a challenging environment for enlightened leadership in a democracy.

The mid-term election of 1994 is my preferred reference point for the start of the Seventh Party System because the startling gains by the Republican Party in the South clearly reflect a culmination of the realignment of white southerners from the Democratic Party to the Republican Party and because the election clearly demonstrates the power of simple populist messaging. In the Senate, Republicans took a 54-46 majority by winning eight seats from Democrats. Tennessee's entire Senate delegation, previously Democrats, were replaced with Republicans. Alabama's Senator Richard Shelby, a long-time Democrat, defected to the Republican Party. In the House of Representatives, Republicans picked up fifty-four seats, including nineteen in the South. For the first time since Reconstruction, there were more Republicans than Democrats representing southern states in the House. The scope of Republican victory, astonishing even for a mid-term election, sprang from the incredibly popular "Contract with America" announced by Republican Newt Gingrich during the campaign.

The realignment of white southerners from the Democratic Party to the Republican Party was motivated to a significant degree by opposition to Democratic support for civil rights and, increasingly, gun control. The realignment began when the Democratic Party led the enactment of the Civil Rights Act of 1964. Less than four months after the Civil Rights Act became law, five states from the south (Louisiana, Mississippi, Alabama, Georgia and South Carolina) supported the Republican Barry Goldwater--who opposed the Civil Rights Act--for president. The only other state Goldwater carried in that election was his home state of Arizona. Before the election of 1964, Democrats held 90 percent of the seats of former confederate states in the House of Representatives. After the dramatic victory for Republicans in the 1994 election, Democrats held only fifty-three percent of seats from these states.

The internet has been the most significant force shaping the Seventh Party System, and the internet enables groups previously unable to coalesce to rally adherents into a politically significant critical mass. Groups with a politically significant critical mass get the attention of politicians, regardless of their agenda. When white southerners first abandoned the Democratic Party in response to the party's support for civil rights legislation, it was still taboo for Republicans to openly court extremist, white nationalist and racist or antisemitic groups. Mainstream Republicans discouraged the political aspirations of David Duke, a former Grand Wizard of the Ku Klux Klan, when Duke switched his party affiliation from Democrat to Republican in 1988. More recently, other domestic extremists like mass-murderer Timothy McVeigh ("Timothy McVeigh...") and the cell that plotted the kidnapping of Michigan governor Gretchen Whitmer in 2020 have aligned with the Republican Party (Mariani). The behavior of some Republican politicians in recent years--addressing gatherings of white nationalists and seeming to tolerate the violent behavior of some white nationalist and neo-Nazi groups--indicates that the realigned Republican Party of the Seventh Party System is now the home of domestic extremism. Some Republican candidates, including the current candidate for President of the United States, appear to court extremism as part of their political brand (Jackson and Coll, Jones).

If I am correct in dating the Seventh Party System to the mid 1990s, then there have been three Republican victories and four Democratic victories in the seven presidential elections during this period. The fact that neither Democrats nor Republicans seem to be dominating the presidential elections in the Seventh Party System is consistent with the idea that information overload has muddled the perceived differences between the parties. In conjunction with the fact that extremist, violent and anti-democratic factions are increasingly accepted as part of the Republican coalition, the lack of understanding of the differences between the parties as they exist today, in the Seventh Party System, and their historical identities is a threat to the survival of the American Republic.

CHAPTER 7

Conclusions and Observations

The analysis of job experience factors in Chapter Two yields three conclusions. The experience factor that makes it most likely to pick a president that ranks in the top third of presidents is experience as a vice president in a prior administration. The next strongest indicator of a candidate likely to rank in the top third of all presidents is experience as the governor of a state or territory. Finally, the factor most likely to result in a candidate ranking in the bottom third of all presidents is the lack of prior experience as an elected public official.

The analysis in Chapter Three highlights at least three common features of our greatest presidents. All of our greatest presidents inspired unity. All of our greatest presidents identified and solved the key crises facing the country while they were in office. All of our greatest presidents left a rich legacy of the words they used to inspire and unite Americans of their era: those words continue to inspire and unite us today.

Our greatest presidents inspired unity. Washington was the only person trusted by all of the factions that threatened to prevent establishment of a successful federal government of the United States. He is the only president unanimously elected by the electoral college, and he was unanimously elected for both his terms. Lincoln's empathy, soaring rhetoric and strong leadership as Commander-in-Chief literally conquered the forces of division and preserved the Union. Teddy Roosevelt inspired unity through his square deal policies that leveraged the federal government to make life fairer for working class Americans. Franklin Roosevelt successfully united Americans across the economic spectrum to meet the challenge of the Great Depression, and then united Americans with a diverse coalition of nations to defeat European fascism and Japanese aggression in the Second World War.

Our greatest presidents identified and successfully resolved the key crises facing the country during their time in office. Washington knew his challenge was keeping the country unified, and his choice of government officials (his cabinet, Supreme Court, etc.) and the procedures he adopted for the executive branch established a tangible sense of national identity that endured over sixty years without civil war, and, when civil war came, was strong enough to survive it. Lincoln was a strong leader who insisted on the indivisibility of the Union, avoided the use of federal force until the South attacked Fort Sumter, and exercised very direct control of the military to achieve total victory. Teddy Roosevelt identified the twin challenges: the global alienation of common people from their government in the industrial era and America's role in the community of nations. He was the first progressive president, and he used the federal government to make American society more fair for the working class. He also did more than any prior president to establish America as a global power: starting the Panama Canal, building up the military, sending the fleet on a tour of the world, and negotiating a treaty to end the Russo-Japanese War. Like Lincoln, Franklin Roosevelt was inaugurated while the country was in the midst of an existential crisis. His bold and immediate actions restored the faith of the people in government and in the economy; within two weeks of his inauguration, Americans had returned one billion dollars to their bank accounts and the stock market had the largest single-day percentage gain in its history (rising over fifteen percent). He proceeded to lead the nation through the Great Depression and in the Second World War.

Our greatest presidents left us a rich legacy of inspirational addresses. When we read the words of Abraham Lincoln during the Civil War, we grasp the empathy of a leader who recognized (and shared) the grief of all Americans for the sacrifices the war demanded, while also illuminating the value of the cause for which those sacrifices were made. Franklin Roosevelt's *First Inaugural Address* reminds us of the enormous suffering caused by unregulated capitalism, and foreshadows the bold action he took to put in place the safeguards we enjoy today. Teddy Roosevelt's inaugural address gives us an example of a leader who is encouraging Americans to be thankful for the legacy left us by the founding generations of our country, while also noting that there are problems we must address together to ensure we leave a like legacy for future generations. Washington's *Farewell Address* is the testimony of the original American superhero to the importance of national unity. Indeed, the words of our greatest presidents in Chapter Five all speak to the power we have when we are united, and to the importance of being diligent in safeguarding that unity. They resonate as well with the confidence and honesty and faith in the American people that have always been the hallmarks of our greatest presidents.

The analysis in Chapter Four tells us our worst presidents have often inspired division and violence. They have often attempted to subvert the proper constitutional decision-making mechanisms in order to assure the outcomes they desired rather than the outcomes that would have come about from the unimpeded operation of those mechanisms. They have sometimes embraced or enabled corruption. They have failed to identify or to successfully overcome the challenge of their time, often because they focused on preserving or restoring some past social system or the nostalgia-infused perception of such a system.

Our worst presidents have often inspired division and violence. Franklin Pierce's persistent use of federal powers to suppress the will of the majority free-staters in Kansas incited violence because it indicated to pro-slavery militias that they could act with impunity while at the same time making free-staters believe they had no recourse but violence. James Buchanan's Kansas policy continued Pierce's failed pro-slavery stance even though the one-sided use of federal power to suppress free-staters was clearly causing violence. The spring of 1858 saw several clashes between federal troops and anti-slavery militias, followed in 1859 by John Brown's raid on the federal armory at Harper's Ferry, Virginia. Andrew Johnson's Reconstruction edicts enabled southern states to establish Black Codes and effectively deny any protection to former slaves, leading to riots in Memphis and New Orleans in 1866 and to more than a century of extra-legal violence against African-Americans by terror groups like the Ku Klux Klan.

Our worst presidents subverted constitutional mechanisms to assure the outcomes they desired, and have sometimes embraced or enabled corruption. James Buchanan, in the months between his election and inauguration, interfered in the Supreme Court's decision process in *Dred Scott versus Sandford*, prevailing upon his fellow Pennsylvanian, Justice Robert C. Grier, to change his dissent to join a majority decision that enabled the Court to rule that Congress could not prohibit slavery in any territory. A Congressional Committee was charged with investigating his administration for widespread corruption, including bribing Members of Congress to vote in favor of the pro-slavery Lecompton Constitution. The Committee's majority report noted significant evidence of corrupt practices, and many of Buchanan's former friends and allies testified against him, but the Committee brought no charges against him. Andrew Johnson was impeached for violating the Tenure of Office Act; he also obstructed congressional efforts to put in place and maintain protections for freed slaves. Warren Harding's administration bred a number of serious corruption scandals, including members of his administration accepting bribes from alcohol bootleggers, oil companies and private persons seeking an inside deal on taking ownership of a German company seized during the First World War. A scandal in the newly formed Veterans Bureau involved the theft of millions by the person Harding put in charge. While Harding was not directly involved in these scandals, he was close friends with some officials ultimately convicted of wrongdoing, and the sheer scale of the corruption indicates he failed in his constitutional duty to ensure faithful execution of the laws.

Our worst presidents failed to identify or to successfully address the major challenges the country faced during their time in office. Pierce failed to chart a course that would avoid civil war, choosing instead to abandon historical precedent and throw the weight of the federal government into supporting the pro-slavery cause in Kansas. Buchanan continued Pierce's disastrous course, and his actions led to escalating violence and secession of several states during his term in office. Andrew Johnson failed to seize the opportunity, granted him by the North's total victory in the Civil War, to impose effective protections for the freed slaves and potentially avoid a century of racial injustice. Warren Harding, pursuing a "return to normalcy", failed to see that America's role in the First World War made returning to pre-war normalcy impossible, and that abdicating America's role in the post-war settlement posed a great risk to the future of America and the world.

We can use what we have learned about the correlation between job experiences and performance as president and about the characteristics of our best and our worst presidents to build a scorecard.

CRITERION	Candidate 1	Candidate 2	COMMENTS
Experience as Vice President in a Prior Administration			
Experience as Governor of State or Territory			
Prior Experience in Government			
Unifier			
Ability to Meet Challenges Facing Country			
Ability to Inspire America			
Divides or Incites Violence			
Fails to Meet Challenge Facing Country			
Corrupt or Shows Lack of Respect for Law/Constitution			

This scorecard can be used in any presidential election. It allows citizens to rate each candidate against the criteria identified in this book for great and poor presidents. Using this tool is one simple way citizens can process the information that bombards us during a presidential election, cut through the marketing tag lines, and make the best possible choice based on substance.

Observations

Applying the criteria we have identified in this book to this year's election is straightforward: for me, the Harris-Walz ticket is a clear winner over Trump-Vance. Here's why:

CRITERION	HARRIS	TRUMP	COMMENTS
Experience as Vice President in a Prior Administration	1	1	Giving Trump benefit of doubt: term as President equivalent
Experience as Governor of State or Territory	0.5	0	Picking Governor as VP counts! Makes stronger ticket.
Prior Experience in Government	1	0.5	Harris Atty Gen, Senator, VP: 15 Trump 1 term President: 4
Unifier	1	0	Harris has significant bipartisan support; Trump does not.
Ability to Meet Challenges Facing Country	?	See Below	
Ability to Inspire America	1	0	First Woman President!
Divides or Incites Violence	NA	-1	Charlottesville riot, G. Floyd riot response, Oct '20 truck incident in Texas, January 6th riot, rhetoric
Fails to Meet Challenge Facing Country	?	-1	Trump failed to meet COVID challenge, costing $$ & lives
Corrupt or Shows Lack of Respect for Law/Constitution	NA	-1	Impeached twice; Attempted to overturn election; Asked for fraud

Criterion 1: Experience as VP in Prior Administration. I gave both tickets a plus 1 here. If experience as a VP in a prior administration has been an indicator of presidential greatness in the past, then experience as president should probably count too, assuming the person who served is not too stupid or proud to learn from their experience. There is only one prior person to serve discontinuous terms as president, so we cannot infer a pattern.

Criterion 2: Experience as Governor of a state or territory. While neither candidate has this experience, the Harris-Walz ticket includes a governor while the Trump-Vance ticket does not, so I gave the Harris-Walz ticket a plus 0.5 for this criterion. Having a former governor as a close advisor in your cabinet is a definite strength.

Criterion 3: Prior Experience in Government (no prior experience correlates with poor performance as president). Trump had this problem in 2016, but since he has one term as president, it no longer applies. I give him a 0.5 here for his four-year term. Harris gets a plus 1 for her fifteen total years as the Attorney General and Senator from California (a state with the fifth largest economy in the world) plus her Vice President time.

Criterion 4: Unifier. Harris gets a plus 1 in this category because, in addition to her widespread popularity among Democrats, she has earned endorsements from over twenty-five prominent Republicans. Harris' GOP endorsements include former Republican governors Weld, Whitman, and Edgar as well as former Members of Congress and former cabinet secretaries. Trump, on the other hand, has only one Democratic endorsement, and that is from former Illinois Governor Rod Blagojevich, who was impeached and imprisoned on federal charges of public corruption for pay-to-play schemes. He was released in 2020 after Trump pardoned him and commuted his sentence.

Criterion 5: Ability to Meet Crisis Facing Our Country. I did not give either candidate a score here. Harris has not had the opportunity to face a crisis in the sense intended here, and I deferred my rating on Trump to Criterion 8, where he loses a point for his failure to successfully meet the COVID crisis.

Criterion 6: Ability to Inspire America. Harris would be the first woman president in American history, more than a century after the Nineteenth Amendment guaranteed women the right to vote. While a candidate's gender is not by itself a reason to vote for (or against) her, the fact that there has never been a woman president of the United States is cause to question the biases inherent in our political systems. Electing our first woman president would be an inspirational event for most Americans, reinforcing the concept of the American dream.

Criterion 7: Divides or Incites Violence. Trump gets a negative 1 in this category for reasons that should be obvious. Far right extremists are part of the current (Seventh Party System) Republican coalition. Here are a few of the well-documented incidents that occurred during his time in office.

(a) In August of 2017, about eight months after Trump was inaugurated, a white nationalist and neo-Nazi rally in Charlottesville to protest the removal of a statue of Robert E. Lee led to a car attack on counter-protesters. A white supremacist named James Fields drove his car into a crowd, killing 32 year-old Heather Heyer and injuring more than thirty others. Three days later, Trump, speaking about the rally, said "I think there is blame on both sides.... you also had people who were very fine people on both sides" (Duggan "Charges upgraded...", Politico staff "Full text: Trump's comments on white supremacists...").

(b) In August of 2019, Patrick Crusius killed 23 people and wounded 22 more in a Walmart in El Paso, Texas. He posted a white nationalist and anti-immigrant statement online shortly before beginning his shooting spree with a legally purchased semi-automatic rifle. The statement uses language that Trump uses, like talking about a migrant invasion. The shooter says that Trump should not be blamed for his (the shooter's) actions, but the shooter was a registered Republican with a Twitter account that featured a picture of Trump in the Oval Office, and he used language that Trump uses when talking about the southern border. Shortly after methodically moving through the store and shooting his victims, Crusius left the scene and surrendered to police. He told police he had targeted Mexicans. He is currently serving ninety life sentences for what has been described as one of the deadliest attacks motivated by white nationalism since the 1995 Oklahoma City bombing that killed 168 men, women and children (*The Guardian*, "El Paso shooting: what we know").

(c) In May of 2020, an unarmed black man named George Floyd was murdered by Minneapolis police officer Derek Chauvin during an arrest. Chauvin, who was ultimately convicted of second degree murder and sentenced to 22 years in prison, was videotaped kneeling on Floyd's neck for several minutes after Floyd said he couldn't breathe and bystanders asked him to stop. Riots quickly spread across the country and the world. While over ninety percent of the protests were peaceful, many included violence, looting and vandalism. The protests, dubbed Black Lives Matter, include about a week of protests near the White House in Washington, D.C. About sixty Secret Service agents were injured in confrontations with rioters, and then President Trump was rushed to the bunker under the White House. According to Reuters, Trump tweeted that any protestors crossing the White House fence would have been "greeted by the most vicious dogs, and the most ominous weapons, I have ever seen." The Mayor of Washington replied with a tweet that there "are no vicious dogs & ominous weapons. There is just a scared man." On June 1, with thousands of additional law enforcement and military personnel deployed in the Washington, D.C. area, officials drew criticism for excessive force when they used tear gas and mounted police to clear peaceful protesters from Lafayette Square so the President and other senior officials could walk over to St John's Episcopal Church (one of the sites that had been damaged by vandalism and arson) for a photograph. By June 4, city officials lifted the curfew (Landay).

(d) On October 30, 2020, a caravan of vehicles carrying Trump campaign flags and sign harassed a Biden campaign bus traveling between San Antonio and Austin. There was a minor collision between one of the Trump supporters' vehicles and a Biden campaign vehicle driving behind the campaign bus. No one was hurt. People on the bus called 911 and canceled the Austin campaign event as a result of this incident. On Saturday, Trump tweeted a video of the incident with the phrase "I LOVE TEXAS!" On Sunday, Trump tweeted, "In my opinion, these patriots did nothing wrong" (Ainsley and Smith).

(e) Joe Biden won the 2020 presidential election with 306 electoral college votes versus 232 for Donald Trump. Nevertheless, Trump immediately and persistently began to argue that the election was stolen, even though he was unable to produce any evidence of the fraud he claimed took place. His own Attorney General, Bill Barr, conducted an investigation that concluded the election was legitimate and that there was no evidence of the fraud that Trump was claiming. Trump's team filed sixty-two lawsuits contesting the results of the election in numerous states, including Arizona, Georgia, Michigan, Nevada, Pennsylvania, Texas and Wisconsin. By November 27, over thirty of these lawsuits had failed. By December 14, over fifty of the lawsuits had been dismissed. Ultimately, all but one of the cases ruled against Trump's allegations. The one suit that initially ruled in his favor in Pennsylvania threw out 2,349 votes, but Trump lost Pennsylvania by 80,355 votes. The Pennsylvania Supreme Court overturned the initial ruling of the court that threw out the 2,349 votes, and reinstated those votes. Sixty-two separate legal proceedings in multiple jurisdictions found Trump's allegations of fraud were unfounded. One judge remarked that "This lawsuit seems to be less about achieving the relief Plaintiffs seek... and more about the impact of their allegations on People's faith in the democratic process and their trust in our government"(Parker, pp. 35-6).

Trump continued to repeat his false claims about the election, especially claiming that Democrats had "rigged" Dominion voting machines to switch votes for Trump to votes for Biden, and that Democrats counted votes by illegal aliens. Although there was no evidence for either claim, Fox News reported the claims as if they were true, deceiving millions of Americans. When Dominion sued Fox News, internal Fox emails showed that the network's executives and anchors were intentionally airing the fake news in order to bolster ratings. Fox News eventually paid Dominion nearly $800 million to settle this case out of court, avoiding a highly public trial (Bauder, Chase and Mulvihill).

Starting in December, Trump tweeted numerous times about the need for a big rally on January 6th to contest the results of the election that he continued to claim was stolen, without any evidence to support his allegations. On January 6th, at the rally he had called for, Trump and a number of people associated with his administration addressed the crowd, which included many members of extremist paramilitary groups. Trump repeated all the false narratives contained in his lawsuits about a stolen election, without regard for the fact that sixty-two independent legal proceedings and his own Attorney General had determined these allegations were baseless. He told the crowd that if they allowed Biden to be certified as president, they would not have a country any more, and that they needed to "fight like hell" to save our democracy. The crowd marched to the Capitol, and a violent riot ensued. Many in the crowd attacked the Capitol police and breached the Capitol building, forcing a delay in the certification procedures. Trump initially refused to make a public call for the crowd to stop what they were doing, even when asked by Republican House Minority Leader Kevin McCarthy (Moe, Jackson, Alba and Clark). Five people were killed and about one-hundred were injured. Trump began to tweet for people to stay peaceful later in the afternoon, after the violence was well underway. Congress reconvened and the certification process took place later that night. On January 13th, the House voted 232 to 197 to impeach Trump for incitement of insurrection. He was acquitted in the Senate.

Criterion 8: Fails to Meet Challenges Facing America. Trump's disastrous failure in meeting the COVID challenge earns him a negative 1 for this criterion. The first case of COVID occurred in the United States and the Republic of Korea (South Korea) on the same day: January 20, 2020. By May 20, Americans were twenty-one times more likely to get the coronavirus and sixty times more likely to die from it than South Koreans.

The difference between the two countries' response to the COVID crisis is a direct reflection of Trump's failure as President. By February 13, South Korea had implemented health screenings for any travelers arriving from countries with reported outbreaks of coronavirus. The South Korean government provided a national hot line number for people experiencing symptoms, and directed those people to an appropriate facility for testing and treatment. By March 23, South Korea had tested nearly 7000 people per million of population as part of a national strategy to identify, contact trace, and contain the virus. In contrast, the United States did not implement health screenings for travelers from countries with coronavirus cases until March 13. By March 23, the United States had tested just over a thousand people per million of population in a largely disjointed effort. Containment and contact tracing were largely left to individual jurisdictions.

The daily intelligence briefings prepared for the president in January and February of 2020 contained numerous warnings about the coronavirus. The Center for Disease Control issued a public notice to hospitals on January 8. Trump did nothing to prepare the country for the virus. Once people started getting sick, he downplayed the seriousness of the crisis. Nearly two weeks after the first case in the United States, he ordered a travel ban from China alone, even though, by that time, other countries had reported cases. On February 26, and said he thought his administration had done a "pretty good job" addressing the crisis. As the situation worsened, he continued to issue inaccurate, self-serving and sometimes harmful statements about the virus. Instead of a coherent national strategy, Trump blamed local and state officials, especially Democrats, for the escalating crisis. On March 24, an Arizona man died after trying to self-medicate with a chemical Trump advocated as a potential cure in a press conference. His wife said "Trump kept saying it was basically pretty much a cure" (CBS News "Arizona Man Dies..."). When his health advisors contradicted him, he demonized them (LaPook). By the end of 2020, nearly 351 thousand Americans had died from coronavirus, making it the third leading cause of death for that year.

Criteria 9: Corrupt or Shows Lack of Respect for Law/Constitution. From the facts presented under Criterion 7, part (d), it should be obvious that Trump lacks respect for the law and the Constitution. I have given him a negative 1 on this criterion, and I will support that by making just three points in addition to the facts presented in Criterion 7, part (d).

The first point is this: The Constitution establishes three co-equal branches of government. The last contested election before 2020 was in 2000, and the election came down to a legal challenge that would award the electors from the state of Florida to either George W. Bush or Al Gore, and that decision would decide who became president. There were a series of court decisions and appeals until ultimately the Supreme Court decided in favor of George W. Bush. Al Gore acknowledged that decision by the judicial branch of government and conceded the race. In the most recent election, which was not decided in just one state, there were 62 separate and independent judgments ruling in favor of Joe Biden, and Donald Trump refused to accept those judicial decisions. He refused to accept the constitutionally established prerogative of the judicial branch.

My second point is that, in addition to being impeached twice for attempting to illegally influence or overturn the 2020 election, Donald Trump has been found guilty in a jury trial of 34 felony counts of falsifying business records to influence the 2016 election by concealing a $130,000 hush money payment to a former porn star with whom he had an affair. A twelve-person jury, selected the way all juries are selected, found Trump guilty. That is the way our system works. Neither Donald Trump nor anyone else gets to keep whining that the system is unfair until they get the decision they want.

My third point is that we have a taped recording of a phone call between then President Trump and several Georgia state officials in which he asks them repeatedly to "find him ... votes". Trump lost Georgia by 11,779 votes, and he asks Georgia state officials to find him the votes he needs to overcome that deficit. He frames his request as a request for the Georgia officials to admit there was fraud, which they repeatedly say is not true, and for which there is no evidence. The case is under investigation by the Fulton County District Attorney (Sherman). In all, prosecutors in seven states--Arizona, Georgia, Michigan, Nevada, New Mexico, Pennsylvania and Wisconsin--have investigated or charged Republican officials with charges relating to a conspiracy to falsely declare Donald

Trump the winner of the 2020 election in those states, to forge documents to that effect, and to transmit those documents to Congress to replace the legitimate electoral documents certified on January 6, 2020. In Arizona, one defendant has pleaded guilty and another has taken a plea deal to support the prosecution's case against others, including former Trump Chief of Staff Mark Meadows and campaign official Rudy Giuliani. In all, at least 84 people have come under investigation in the fake elector plot (O'Driscoll).

In sum, then, the Harris-Walz ticket scores 4.5 on the scorecard, while Trump-Vance scores negative 1.5. In my view, and I believe the overwhelming weight of evidence supports this view, Donald Trump was a failure in his first term. In spite of the fact that Republicans controlled both the House and the Senate from 2016 to 2018, he was unable to get an infrastructure bill passed, he failed to reduce the deficit in the federal budget, and he failed to enact any lasting immigration reform or border security measures. Most importantly, as described above, his failure to successfully address the defining crisis of his presidency--the COVID pandemic--and his insistence on the false narrative that he won the 2020 election (he is recently on the record admitting that he lost) give him more in common with our worst presidents than with our best presidents.

WORKS CITED

Ainsley, Julia and Allan Smith. "Trump responds after FBI investigating harassment of Biden campaign bus in Texas". NBC News, www.nbcnews.com/politics/2020-election/live-blog/2020-11-01-trump-biden-election-n1245634#ncrd1245722, Nov 1, 2020.

APSA. https://en.wikipedia.org/wiki/Historical_rankings_of_presidents_of_the_United_States#Scholar_survey_summary.

Baker, Jean H. *James Buchanan*. Times Books, Henry Holt and Company, 2004, New York.

Bauder, David, with Randall Chase and Geoff Mulvihill. "Fox, Dominion reach $787 Million Settlement Over Election Claims". Associated Press, apnews.com/article/fox-news-dominion-lawsuit-trial-trump-2020-0ac71f75acfacc52ea80b3e747fb0afe, April 18, 2023.

Brands, H.W. *Traitor to His Class: The Privileged Life and Radical Presidency of Franklin Delano Roosevelt*. Anchor Books, 2008, New York, NY.

Brooks, Emily. "Johnson: 'Now is not 'the time for comprehensive immigration reform'". thehill.com/homenews/house/4413501-mike-johnson-immigration-reform/amp/, January 17, 2024.

WORKS CITED

Cassatta, Donna. "Boehner: No Formal Talks on Immigration Bill". apnews.com/article/5dd69281d5dc4728b676cbfeb87eacf8; November 13, 2013.

CBS News. 'Arizona man dies, wife ill after taking drug touted as virus treatment: "Trump kept saying it was basically pretty much a cure"'.www.cbsnews.com/news/coronavirus-news-arizona-man-dies-after-taking-chloroquine-drug-touted-by-trump-as-treatment/, March 24, 2020.

Cheney, Kyle and Josh Gerstein. "Federal judges reject GOP effort to overturn swing state election results". www.politico.com/news/2020/12/07/judge-rejects-overturn-michigan-election-results-443411, December 7, 2020.

CSPAN. https://www.c-span.org/presidentsurvey2021/.

"Democratic Party Platform 1980". The American Presidency Project, www.presidency.ucsb.edu/documents/1980-democratic-party-platform.

Duggan, Paul. "Charge upgraded to first-degree murder for driver accused of ramming Charlottesville crowd". *The Washington Post*, www.washingtonpost.com/local/crime/driver-accused-of-plowing-into-charlottesville-crowd-killing-heather-heyer-due-in-court/2017/12/13/6cbb4ce8-e029-11e7-89e8-edec16379010_story.html, December 14, 2017.

Fauci, Anthony. "Statement on hydroxychloroquine". CBS, x.com/CBSEveningNews/status/1241041232421433345?s=20.

Federalist. web.archive.org/web/20060207050558/http://www.opinionjournal.com/extra/?id=110007243.

Goodwin, Doris Kearns. *No Ordinary Time Franklin & Eleanor Roosevelt: The Home Front in World War II*. Simon & Schuster, 1994, New York, NY.

Goodwin, Doris Kearns. *Team of Rivals*. Simon & Schuster, 2005, New York, NY.

Jackson, Rebecca and Steve Coll. "How the Proud Boys are prepping for a second Trump term". *The Economist*, www.economist.com/1843/2024/07/22/how-the-proud-boys-are-prepping-for-a-second-trump-term, July 22, 2024.

Jones, Ja'han. "Many years after the Oklahoma City bombing, Republicans have learned the wrong lessons". MSN, www.msn.com/en-us/news/us/many-years-after-the-oklahoma-city-bombing-republicans-have-learned-the-wrong-lessons/ar-AA1nic5y?ocid=feedsansarticle, April 19, 2024.

Kapur, Sahil and Scott Wong, Julie Tsirkin, Julia Ainsley. "Senators unveil bipartisan bill to impose tougher asylum and border laws". NBC News, www.nbcnews.com/politics/congress/new-immigration-asylum-reform-bill-released-senate-text-rcna136602, February 4, 2024.

Landay, Jonathan. "Trump says protesters would have met 'vicious dogs' if White House fence breached". Reuters, www.reuters.com/article/us-minneapolis-police-protests-trump/trump-says-protesters-would-have-met-vicious-dogs-if-white-house-fence-breached-idUSKBN2360LJ/, May 30, 2020.

Lapook, Jon. "Fauci admits administration has restricted his media appearances, says he's not surprised Trump got COVID". CBS News, www.cbsnews.com/news/fauci-no-surprised-trump-covid-19-media-appearances-60-minutes/, October 19, 2020.

WORKS CITED

Lincoln, Abraham. "First Inaugural Address". www.loc.gov/exhibits/lincoln/ext/transcription14.html.

Lincoln, Abraham. "The Gettysburg Address". www.loc.gov/resource/rbpe.244045-00/?st=text

Lincoln, Abraham. "1863 State of the Union Address". www.infoplease.com/primary-sources/government/presidential-speeches/state-union-address-abraham-lincoln-december-8-1863

Lincoln, Abraham. "Second Inaugural Address". www.loc.gov/resource/lprbscsm.sc- sm-0304/

Mariani, Mack. "The Michigan militia: Political engagement or political alienation?". *Terrorism and Political Violence* Volume 10 1998, Issue 4, www.tandfonline.com/doi/abs/10.1080/09546559808427485.

Marquez, Alexandra. "Trump acknowledges losing the 2020 election 'by a whisker'". www.nbcnews.com/news/amp/rcna169526, September 4, 2024.

McCullough, David. *Mornings on Horseback The Story of an Extraordinary Family, a Vanished Way of Life, and the Unique Child Who Became Theodore Roosevelt.* Simon & Schuster, 1981, New York, NY.

Moe, Alex, and Hallie Jackson, Monica Alba, Dartunorro Clark. "McCarthy and Trump got into an expletive-filled argument during Capitol riot, sources say". NBC News, www.nbcnews.com/politics/donald-trump/mccarthy-trump-got-expletive-filled-argument-during-capitol-riots-sources-n1257805, February 12, 2021.

Naylor, Brian. "Read Trump's Jan. 6 Speech, A Key Part of Impeachment Trial". NPR, www.npr.org/2021/02/10/966396848/read-trumps-jan-6-speech-a-key-part-of-impeachment-trial, February 10, 2021.

O'Driscoll, Sean. "Dominoes Are Falling in Arizona False Electors Case". Newsweek, www.newsweek.com/donald-trump-jenna-ellis-arizona-plea-agreement-pelligrino-court-1935995, August 7, 2024.

Parker, the Honorable Linda V. "OPINION AND ORDER DENYING PLAINTIFFS' "EMERGENCY MOTION FOR DECLARATORY, EMERGENCY, AND PERMANENT INJUNCTIVE RELIEF" (ECF NO. 7). " United States District Court, Eastern District of Michigan, Southern Division. storage.courtlistener.com/recap/gov.uscourts.mied.350905/gov.uscourts.mied.350905.62.0_3.pdf, December 7, 2020.

Peller, Lauren. "'Even Worse Than We Expected': House Speaker Reacts to Bipartisan Senate Immigration Bill". abcnews.go.com/Politics/speaker-mike-johnson-house-gop-members-react-bipartisan/story?id=106944092, February 24, 2024.

Politico staff. "Full text: Trump's comments on white supremacists, 'alt-left' in Charlottesville". Politico, www.politico.com/story/2017/08/15/full-text-trump-comments-white-supremacists-alt-left-transcript-241662, August 15, 2017.

Potter, David Morris. *The Impending Crisis, 1848-1861*. Harper & Row, 1976.

"Report of the Joint Committee on Reconstruction". www.senate.gov/artandhistory/history/resources/pdf/JointCommitteeonReconstruction1866.pdf

"Republican Party Platform 1980". The American Presidency Project, www.presidency.ucsb.edu/documents/republican-party-platform-1980.

WORKS CITED

Roosevelt, Franklin Delano. "First Inaugural Address". www.archives.gov/educa-tion/lessons/fdr-inaugural

Roosevelt, Theodore. "Inaugural Address". www.loc.gov/item/pin3501/

SCRI. https://en.wikipedia.org/wiki/Historical_rankings_of_presidents_of_the_United_States#Scholar_survey_summary.

Shabad, Rebecca and Monica Alba. "Trump calls Fauci a 'disaster' and says it would be a 'bomb' if he fired him". NBC News, www.nbcnews.com/politics/politics-news/fauci-says-he-s-not-surprised-trump-contracted-covid-19-n1243857, October 19, 2020.

Sherman, Amy. "Here's what Donald Trump asked Georgia election officials in phone call about 2020 election". www.politifact.com/article/2023/jul/25/heres-what-donald-trump-asked-georgia-election-off/. July 25, 2023.

"The Civil War: The Senate's Story: Victory, Tragedy and Reconstruction". www.senate.gov/artandhistory/history/common/civil_war/VictoryTragedyReconstruction.htm

The Constitution of the United States with Index and *The Declaration of Independence.* House Document 112-129, Twenty-Fifth Edition (House Concurrent Resolution 90), 2012.

The Guardian, https://www.theguardian.com/us-news/2019/aug/03/el-paso-shooting-what-we-know-so-far

"Timothy McVeigh: Convicted Oklahoma City Bomber". Cable News Network (CNN), web.archive.org/web/20060209045752/http://archives.cnn.com/2001/US/03/29/profile.mcveigh/, March 29, 2001.

Tuchman, Barbara. *The Proud Tower: A Portrait of the World Before the War, 1890-1914.* Random House, 1962, New York.

Washington, George. "The Farewell Address". founders.archives.gov/documents/Washington/05-20-02-0440-0002

www.ingramcontent.com/pod-product-compliance
Lightning Source LLC
Chambersburg PA
CBHW060514030426
42337CB00015B/1886